A Paper Route
is good for the Soul

Riley B. Case

A Paper Route is good for the Soul

ISBN: 978-1-60920-003-9
Printed in the United States of America
©2010 by Riley B. Case

Cover and interior design by Isaac Publishing, Inc.
Photographs property of author

Library of Congress Cataloging-in-Publication Data

Isaac Publishing, Inc.
P.O. 342
Three Rivers, MI 49093
www.isaacpublishing.com

Please direct your inquiries to admin@isaacpublishing.com

A Paper Route
is good for the Soul

Riley B. Case

Isaac Publishing, Inc.
www.isaacpublishing.com

Contents

Foreword

This book is a collection of autobiographical essays written over a period of a number of years. There were a number of different audiences in mind when I wrote them, and they were written for a number of different occasions. There is no connecting theme to the essays, nor any sequential order. The content is not much like some of the other things I have written. For example, there is nothing much (at least directly) about the history and/or the politics of the United Methodist Church, about United Methodist General Conferences, nor about what bishops ought to be doing these days, matters I have written about elsewhere.

Rather these are more like reflections on church, family, and experiences that meant something to me. I guess I hoped that at least my family might be interested in them. Perhaps persons from LaGrange or Berne or North Dakota or Taylor University might find those chapters worth reading.

The first essay written was "I Never Owned a Gun," after I had a class on the prophets at Garrett Biblical Institute taught by John Miller (he was an adjunct professor who had studied under Karl Barth) of Reba Place (a gathered Anabaptist community in Evanston, Illinois). About the same time I did a sociological research paper on Berne, Indiana, one of the more fascinating places I had any acquaintance with. Among the findings: in the 1950s the average worship attendance of the several churches in the community was greater than the population of the town.

So I wrote, "I Never Owned a Gun," thinking I might try to have it published, if for no other reason than to tell an interesting story, and also to make a point that not all evangelicals are warmongers.

Some years later I then wrote "The Messiah and Mennonite Evangelism," which was also a story about Berne.

The essay "A Paper Route is Good for the Soul" was written in the 1970s when I needed to do a program for some group. I shared an experience that had been held private for many years. It, along with most of the stories, was written to be read, or at least told, and that is reflected by the writing style. The same is true with "Nothing Among You Save Jesus Christ," which has been a good story for gatherings of pastors and others who love small churches. A companion piece, "The Blood-Washed Banner of Holiness" was another story for preachers, but I used it also as a lead story for my book, *Evangelical and Methodist A Popular History*. The essay on my friend Luther, "You Cut Down my Tomatoes," has been used in sermons and/or as a devotional. The story "Three by the Stork, One by United" was also an expansion of a sermon illustration (love as a gift). I wrote and used the essay on "The LaGrange School" when I spoke at the LaGrange alumni banquet one year.

Of course I needed to say something about North Dakota and my wife Ruth, and so I wrote about the day in September when I went to North Dakota for the first time. That would be the account titled "The Ring Was in the Pocket." "The Killdeers Are Back" is also a North Dakota story which I first wrote in part in "The Circuit," a round-robin letter which I participated in with Taylor University friends for a number of years. It was the sharing with friends of a meaningful spiritual experience. Taylor friends were also in mind in the account of "She Was a Calvinist Anyway," which is a personal account of my year in Swallow-Robin dorm at Taylor. Others have their own stories about that Swallow-Robin year and these will be told at the 1952-53 Swallow Robin reunion which is planned for October, 2010 at Taylor.

I wrote about my father ("Riley Leander Case 1896-1988") as a tribute to him after his death. Later I did the essay on my mother, "Brown Spots and Blue Birds"). Of course I then needed to add the chapter related to both of those chapters which was "711 Hawpatch."

I express thanks to my wife Ruth, who shared a number of these experiences with me, to my children, Cristin, Jay, Jeremy, and Karen, for their willingness to listen to some of these stories before they were ever put on paper, and to my other friends and relatives who have helped to make life interesting.

A Paper Route Is Good For The Soul

Written in the 1970s

A paper route is good for the soul. My sons insist their paper routes were not good for their souls; but since they are under thirty, their judgment is impaired. Middle-aged men cooped up behind desks, far removed from wet shoes, barking dogs, and ladies who never have change—they are best qualified to reflect on the spiritual values of paper routes.

Ted Groat, Beaver Patrol leader, who did the sales job on me to take the route when I was fourteen, did not mention spiritual values, as I recall. He mentioned money: forty-five customers times seven and a half cents a customer. Then in language which prefigured Methodist district superintendent speeches later to come, he spoke of a "challenge," and a "great opportunity."

On the scale of life's priorities, at least as perceived at that time, the paper route was somewhere down the list, along with brushing teeth and the Restoration of Europe. In my faithfully kept diary it hardly rated mention except on the days I "froze to death" or "drowned in the rain." Otherwise, the diary was filled with entries describing baseball games heard over the radio and when baths were taken. Like the many unremembered diaries down through the ages, it also noted whether it was rainy or sunny.

But nostalgia and the human spirit have a way of sorting things out. Today the baseball games and baths have faded into obscurity. And in their place (in those unsolicited daydreams that so often interrupt sermon-making) are long-ago conversations around the

supper table, impressions of neighbors who lived down the street—
and the paper route.

Expecially the paper route. I associate it with the crunch of fall
leaves under a bicycle tire, with the fresh smell of warmed earth in
spring, with trampling through snow and the setting sun on cold
winter evenings, with riding home on Hawpatch Street and feeling
good about a job done.

My territory was North Poplar Street and points east. I knew the
dogs and squirrels there. I knew which maple trees turned reddest
in the fall. I knew where the mysterious power of tree roots made
sidewalks heave and bicycle riding dangerous. I knew the homes that
smelled like cooked cabbage on the inside. I knew where you could
find Christmas decorations still up in the middle of January.

I set new world's records for that paper route: the world's fastest
time on a bike…while walking…with the help of mother's car. I
set the world's record for distance a paper could be thrown from a
bicycle…while walking…left handed.

I engineered shortcuts and platted trails. That is I did until one
day until Mr. Sherman asked me what in the world was going on
with those bicycle marks across his lawn. (No answer) Whatever it
was I was not to do it any more because people do not like bicycle
trails through their lawns (a thought that had not occurred to me).

Delivering papers was sometimes accompanied with play-by-play
commentary suitable for the National Broadcasting Company: "….no
use taking the driveway, he'll jump the curb…a beautiful job…but
can he make the throw?…Yes! Well, maybe yes…Will they find the
paper? And now for the real test…Henry, the mad dog…That paper
boy is a champion…one kick and that dog runs for home…"

The commentary, the world's records, the doing of battle with
dogs, the weather, cantankerous customers, the mystery of the insides
of people's houses—all of this was a private world, not shared with
friends, relatives, or even parents.

The paper route introduced me to the wonders of the universe.
The customer Nelson was really the proprietor of a nursing home,
or nursing house. The house was the place of the living dead, old
women lying unmoving in beds close together, old men sitting

motionless with spittoons at their feet. The odor was unbearable. When I collected I set a world's record for holding my breath while discussing the weather and waiting for Mrs. Nelson to find the proper change.

The customer known as Campbell was an even greater mystery. It wasn't much of a house: mostly one room with the bed and the davenport and the kitchen table all together. The furniture had to share space with beer bottles. Collecting there meant going through a ritual. Pounding. More pounding. Sometimes no answer. Sometimes creaking bedsprings; and this at 10:00 on Saturday morning. The door would open and I would give my speech: I was the paper boy (they seemed to forget from week to week) and no, they hadn't paid last week nor the week before.

They had the money, usually, providing they could find Mr. Campbell's pants. That was no easy task: they had to sort through children's toys, dirty clothes, diapers, dishes, paper; left-over food was scattered helter skelter; but mostly there were beer bottles—on the table, on the floor, on the couch, upright, on their side, rolling around. A world's record for beer bottles in one house. Sometimes they asked me in while they looked. I tried not to stare. For years my concept of a hang-over was a half-naked blurry-eyed man, and sometimes a half-naked blurry-eyed woman, scrounging for some lost pants in a one-room house among the beer bottles while the paper boy looked on.

But it is about another customer that this chapter is written.

One very cold, winter day, I was coasting down Steuben Street and had just hit the railroad tracks (at an inordinate rate of speed), when I heard a loud "Hey!"

There was no one to connect the voice to. It was like out of heaven—or someplace else. Furthermore, it was not a friendly "Hey," as in "My friend, what are you doing in a place like this?" It was a stop-right-now kind of "Hey," as in "What are you doing on my lawn?" or, "stop in the name of the law!" I set a world's record for rate of speed on a bicycle down Steuben Street.

When I reached the bottom of the hill I looked back.

It was a witch. A woman all in black in the underbrush by an abandoned shack. There may have been a logical explanation for it all, but I was determined not to find out what it was.

A few days later the "Hey" came again. This time I saw her, and she saw that I saw her. I debated with myself about stopping, and lost. I was not raised to ignore "Heys."

She *was* a witch. At least she came close, if appearances counted for anything. Old, short, stooped, with teeth missing, and a sharp jaw. Her face was dirty, like in pictures of coal miners. From shawl to shoes, she was black. She had a cigarette in her mouth, a crutch in one arm, and a pan of ashes in the other.

"Would you carry these ashes out to that ash pile for me?" The path to the ash pile was icy. In a way the question was a relief. I was not going to be lectured about riding too fast down the hill, or kicking at dogs, or allowing papers to blow all over the neighborhood. The ashes were carried and I was gone.

But that was by no means the end. She was there again, a few days later. Nothing had changed—dirty face, crutch, ashes, icy path. Except maybe the cigarette was shorter. The ashes were right at the lips, curled and ready to fall. They fell, but she noticed not at all. I stared. Mrs. Campbell, half-dressed, hair disheveled, looking for her husband's pants under beer bottles, could smoke. That seemed fitting. But an old lady, with a crutch and a pan of ashes on an icy path? Smoking? To my Methodist eyes it was not fitting.

This time it was not just carry out the ashes but would I also pump some water into a pail. I tried to figure out what was happening. The abandoned shack was obviously not abandoned. This old lady lived there—crippled, dirty, and ---to my horror---shivering. She wore no gloves, no boots, no coat, and it was cold.

Perhaps from habit, perhaps to remind her that I didn't ride down Steuben Street day after day just to look for ashes to carry out, I mentioned that I delivered the *Fort Wayne News-Sentinel*. Then in a bit of reckless abandon, I asked her if she would like to subscribe. I could imagine no prospect less likely.

"How much?" I couldn't believe her answer and had to ask her what she said.

"How much?" That definitely was a sign of interest.

"Twenty-five cents a week."

She would subscribe.

Astonishment. "When should I start?"

"Tomorrow."

What was her name?

"Maude Callahan."

"Where should I leave her paper?" I forsaw a problem: there was no big porch to throw a paper on. Nor a little porch. There was no porch at all. Not even a respectable step. Nor a screen door. Nor a mail box that I could see.

She said something about knocking on the door.

The next day I knocked. And knocked. There was a long wait while, amid groans and grunts and thumping of the crutch and the barking of a dog and remarks to someone (it turned out to be the dog), Mrs. Callahan slowly and torturously made her way to the door. I wondered how many boys in LaGrange, Indiana, or in the whole world for that matter, knocked on the door and hand-delivered the evening paper.

The thumping stopped. "Who is it?"

I explained I was the paper boy and she said yesterday she would subscribe to the *News Sentinel*. The latch clicked, and Mrs. Callahan said, "Come in."

What now? This was much to elaborate a ritual just to deliver a paper for 7.5 cents profit per week. If this was to be a pattern all world records for speed in delivering papers would never again be broken.

Furthermore, I wasn't sure what would be inside. The witch image was still there and the whole business looked suspiciously like some variation on Hansel and Gretel. But that also made for curiosity and adventure.

I went in. I did not suspect that moment would be remembered so vividly in years to come.

On the floor in front, in the middle of the "kitchen," was a pile of coal. To the right was a table stacked with a variety of discolored containers and food, or what was left of it. The floor was rough and bare and dirty, as were the walls, the ceiling, the windows, and everything else. The rest seemed to be boxes, trash, dark corners, and cobwebs. The smell was worse than that at the nursing home. One of its components was the reminders of an untrained dog. There was no heat.

Mrs. Callahan gave me to know I was to follow, groans, tapping crutch, and all, and so I did. By way of a certain path because, as she explained, the floor was"giving way" over on one side. There was some panic in the contemplation of what the floor might give way to. For all I knew it was a bottomless pit.

The next room, or "front room," was more of the same, except in the center there was a rocking chair and a table with lamp and radio and numerous other things of a nondescript nature. Next to the chair was a pot-bellied stove. This was where Mrs. Callahan lived. She sat down—finally—and I delivered to her the paper. The ritual was to be repeated many times in coming months.

We began to talk. She because she was lonely. I because I had just been ushered into the eighth wonder of the world and I was consumed by curiousity. That this house existed, that this lady lived in LaGrange, Indiana, just yards from the path I traveled every day, unknown to me and, I was sure, unknown to the whole world, was an incomprehensible mystery. It was like an Alice in Wonderland tunnel to a different world. Before I left I carried out more ashes.

The next day was the same. And the day after that. And the day after that. At first the conversation was polite. We spoke of her dog and the stove and my paper route. I carried ashes and pumped water. One day there was a letter in tortured handwriting for the box by the street to the grocery store. The tasks were not hard. Years later it occurred to me I was spared the trauma of emptying the bed pan. I had seen it on occasions. There was, lost in the underbrush, an outdoor privy, but it was not used.

The conversation became more personal. She spoke of places and people and family and incidents of long ago. Something about a farm and work and an automobile accident. Someone pictured in an old, dusty frame hanging on the wall was part of the stories. In return I told of my "people," and my sisters and raising chickens and church. For once major league baseball was irrelevant.

I asked questions. Where were her children…did they ever come to see her…had she ever thought of living with them…who did come to see her…how did she shop…did she ever go anyplace?

Her children were off someplace…she seldom saw them…it would not work to live with them…she did not shop…the coal man delivered coal and the grocery man her groceries…she did not see her neighbors…the lady from the welfare office stopped to see her every so often.

More questions and answers. She lived on eighteen dollars a month—from welfare. She had not been in her basement for quite a few years. There was still some canned food down there. (I wondered if antique canned food was still good to eat.) She had not been uptown for—how long?—maybe twelve years.

The twelve years did it. This was unimaginable cultural deprivation. Not to have seen up-town LaGrange—the Amish buggies, the court house, Brown's Drug Store—for twelve years! Alas! Maude was prisoner in her own home, in a cell with dirt and smell and cold.

And Maude was poor. I was convinced. Really poor. Poor like we read about in Sunday school lessons and heard about in sermons (it strikes me now that we never discussed such things in school). Poor like people who had to go to the poor farm (I never knew what the poor farm was but from reading books I knew it was a fate worse than death). Poor like boys in Horatio Alger books from Grandpa Case's bookcase.

Some of the kids at school were kind-of poor. At least we sometimes suspected. Their hair grew down over their ears before they got haircuts. They wore overalls to school (and were envied by those of us who had to wear corduroys). They brought lunches instead of eating in the cafeteria.

But they were hardly poor like Maude. I thought about it. I thought about it a lot. It became a "burden". And a burden, in my developing evangelical world, was a religious thing.

I do not now, years later, remember that I often thought in religious terms at that age. I did not doubt my faith. My Aunt Selma always told me I accepted Jesus at age three. That was enough evidence for me whenever salvation was questioned. I was always in church.

But that did not mean I was greatly impressed by matters of the Spirit. In the worship services in the summer I worked on projects like establishing the world's record for number of flies that could be caught by hand in one hour. I made mental notes that sermons in Mennonite churches were longer than sermons in Methodist churches. I was not sure of any great connection between what went on in church and what went on in the rest of the world.

But with Maude the connection was made. When I thought of Maude being poor I thought religiously.

I thought of Jesus and the beggars, and the crippled man on his pallet and the man who fell among thieves and how Jesus said, "Blessed are the poor." I thought of helping and witnessing and heaven and hell. God loved Maude. I was not particularly conscious that God loved the Campbells with all their beer bottles, but I believed God loved Maude.

Did Maude go to church? I asked her that one day, despite the fact that she had not been uptown for twelve years. Had she ever gone to church? She mentioned that years before some people used to pick her up and take her. "What church?" I suspected it was not the Methodist Church. It wasn't. It was the Church of God. My estimation of the Church of God went up several notches. Did she believe in God? She did. I wanted to press that further but I didn't know how.

For a while I thought Maude might like to visit the Methodist Church. It was a depressing revelation when I realized that people like Maude didn't attend the Methodist Church. Even cleaned up it wouldn't work. My Christian zeal was facing reality.

I then had the idea my parents could take Maude for a car ride around town. At least Maude could see the Methodist Church, and the court house, and the Amish buggies and Brown's Drug Store. To my surprise neither Maude nor my mother was much excited about it.

Unfortunately, I had never shared at home about the Maude part of my life. My mother had asked why I was getting home later from my paper route. I explained that I had a new customer and I was carrying out ashes and pumping water. It was a woman.

A woman? Mother was suspicious, and then alarmed. Years later I understood the reason for alarm. Her son spending time with some woman in the woman's home? Helping? Helping? It is true I had not distinguished myself at home as one who ordinarily out of the love of my heart did household tasks for others. If mother's love and scolding could hardly get me to dry dishes, how was I about to carry out ashes for some woman on the other side of town?

When mother took me on my route one evening in the car, her alarm become something like panic. The outside of the shack seemed much too sinister for her. I knew in a moment it would never do for her to see the inside of the shack, or to be approached about Maude's grand sight-seeing tour around the city of LaGrange, Indiana, population 1812. It would be best if Maude and my mother never met.

That represented a setback. The Methodist Church and my mother had now been eliminated as possible allies in the crusade for social justice. I turned next to the neighbors. With a boldness that amazes me now, years later, I approached several neighbors, good customers all.

Did they know the old lady, Mrs. Callahan, who lived in the house over there? Did they know anything about her children? Did they ever visit her? Did they ever see her? Did anyone ever see her?

They knew about Maude. She didn't get along with her children. The place is filthy. She is filthy. She sticks to herself. Someone from welfare stops in. Stay away. She's trouble.

So much for the neighbors.

Next was the welfare lady. I met her one day as I was arriving at Maude's. I asked her what was going to happen to Maude. She probably wondered who was I to be asking such questions. She was vague. Maude could go to the county farm, or to her children's, but she didn't want to.

I knew that already.

No help from the Methodist Church, nor my mother, nor the neighbors, nor the welfare lady.

Meanwhile the routine continued. A knock at the door, grunts, groans, tapping of the crutch, angry remarks to the dog. The latch undone and the invitation to come in. I didn't go in every day. Sometimes I just handed her the paper, asked if she needed anything done, and told her I was in a hurry. Sometimes when I went in I sat down. Conversation was never hard, even when basketball and baseball were excluded as topics. Sometimes we talked about God and the church. Sometimes she talked about things she heard over the radio and things happening around town.

Christmas came. A paperboy's favorite time. There were tips and presents from customers. Candy, oranges, gum, cards. Raymond and I fixed a box for Maude. Raymond was my friend and substitute and the only other person who really knew about Maude.

I am not sure how or when we decided on the basket. I don't remember what was in our minds. In those days I didn't question motives and analyze motives behind motives. "If your eye be single…" I don't remember even what was in the box. Some food, of course, and other things. It was delivered in the evening, after papers had been delivered. I think on Christmas Eve.

In the years since there have been many baskets. They are filled with clothes and food, at Christmas or Thanksgiving, and given on behalf of the church, or a class in the church. Giving baskets has not always been enjoyable work. It accentuates the poverty. It draws more sharply the line between the haves and have-nots. The receivers are sometimes resentful that their misfortune has been placed on public view. The givers expect gratitude. Baskets are often delivered quickly, business-like, with a minimum of conversation.

It was not so with Maude's Christmas basket. It was delivered with care. I remember I really wanted to go, and the giving was easy. It was not at the usual paper route time. It was later, after supper.

Maude was surprised. It was an unexpected visit, totally unexpected. I gave her the basket. She was moved. There was a crack in the hard crust. Her voice broke. Maude seldom showed emotion. If there was discouragement, joy, anger, sadness, love, it was all buried underneath. But on the day of the Christmas basket, it showed.

After a silence she asked, "Why are you boys so nice to me?

It was my turn to be surprised. It was a personal question.

The kind that teen-age boys avoid, when possible. I said the first thing that came to my mind: "They teach us at church to love one another."

I was embarrassed to have said it. It was a religious explanation for an act not consciously conceived as religious. I do not remember thinking, "It is Christmas time and in order to be good Methodists we should remember the poor."

But maybe that is the way it is supposed to be. Didn't the righteous say in the parable, "Lord, when did we see thee hungry...?" And the Lord's reply, "Inasmuch as you have done it unto one of the least of these..." For once in my life, maybe it was the first, maybe the only time, the love was unmotivated. I was not conscious of wanting to impress parents or friends or the pastor, or even God.

The scene will be forever impressed on my mind. I'm sure it moves me now more than it did then, originally. Dim light from shaded light bulb. A pot-bellied stove. Ashes, dirt, and dog droppings littering the floor. A long silence, perhaps because no words seemed quite appropriate. I believe it reminded me of a stable. The basket was the only reminder of Christmas. No decorations, no cards, no other presents. Tomorrow, at my parent's home, there would be laughing and singing and eating. There would be presents and lights and warmth. Maude's day would be like any other days, except there would not even be the *News Sentinel* to read. There was a lump in my throat.

The Christmas card that had been in the basket lay on Maude's table for months after that. One day there was with it a newspaper clipping with my picture in it. It was for something or other, maybe 4-H. Maude had cut it out and stuck it on her radio. I asked why the clipping. She said she wanted to be reminded of her paper boy.

I saw less of Maude in the months following. Raymond handled the route more often and when he couldn't there were other substitutes. Basketball, work, things at school, even girls, took more of my time.

One day one of the substitutes announced that Maude was gone. He was told she was going to live with her daughter. He didn't know where the daughter lived.

Months went by. One day Raymond announced he had directions to Maude's daughter's house. Somebody knew somebody who worked at the welfare office. It was north of Middlebury, maybe twenty-five miles away. We were both driving by then. We went on a Saturday. We found a basement home on a country road.

We knocked. There was a sound inside. We opened the door and asked if this is where Maude Callahan was staying. The voice said, "Come downstairs." A woman was at the foot of the stairs.

"Are you Maude?" It was not a greeting. It was a question for information. She was different, very different. The face was full and clean and wrinkled (the wrinkles had not shown through dirt). Her hair was white. She wore a print dress. I'm not sure why I had expected to see her same dirty hair and black dress. She had gained weight. She was younger than I had thought. Maybe in her late sixties. The witch image was gone.

But of course she would be different! She was being cared for. She was eating. She looked good. Raymond and I both remarked that she looked good. How was she getting along? How is she liking it?

Then came the great disappointment. Maybe we expected too much. Obviously the setting was different. The dog was gone. And the pot-bellied stove. And the shack. Raymond and I were both older, and taller. We must have looked strange to Maude.

Maude answered our questions. She talked. But it was different. Not until later, much later, did I realize what was so different. Maude was whining. In the voice was self-pity. In years to come I would hear it many times—in nursing homes, hospitals, dingy apartments, in dark Victorian homes--the widowed, the aged, those for whom purposeful work and useful like is in the past. Growing old without grace and dignity.

She laid out her grievances like we were counselors. She should have never come…She missed her dog…Like now, the rest of the people usually gone…The granddaughter made too much noise… They did not like her radio…She did not have a room of her own… She could not climb the stairs…There was nothing to do…

I was confused. I had wanted this to happen for Maude's sake. I had wanted her to be warm and well-fed and cared for. I had wanted her to be clean and with people. I did not want her to be poor. It had never occurred to me it might not work, that something would be lost in leaving the shack. And now, we all knew, there was no going back.

We finally left. We said to her, and to ourselves, we would be back. We never made it.

I used to pray for Maude. I still do occasionally, and wonder about it since my theology does not encourage prayers for the dead, and it has been so many years ago. I am reminded of her, every so often: during a visit to a nursing home, or a conversation with an elderly widow, listening to stories of family and farms and events that took place long ago. Especially I am reminded when the paper boy collects at Christmas. I think of the old paper route, of the Christmas box, of Jesus, and the poor, and of Maude.

I Never Owned A Gun

I never owned a gun. I played with pretend guns in the pasture. One pretend-gun was a store-bought cowboy six-shooter, given as a birthday present--I don't remember from whom. Later it disappeared. On another occasion, when I had money, I bought a cap pistol and had it for awhile. But I never owned a real gun, like an air pistol, or a BB gun, or a twenty-two.

My friends did. In lower grades they had enough toy weapons to start a revolution. In junior high they plugged birds and squirrels and cans off the back fence with BB guns. In high school they stalked ducks and rabbits and argued the merits of different gauged shotguns. But I was silent, for I never owned a gun.

Japs and Germans were coming in those days—during World War II—and guns were what we were going to use to save the world, along with tanks and fighter planes and submarines. We kept the effort alive on the home front by singing war songs in music class and by using school time to walk the two blocks to the post office to exchange dimes for war stamps.

Buy some, buy some, buy some right today.
Buy some, buy some, keep the Japs away.

We cheered our war heroes in comic books and fought Hitler by cleaning the macaroni and cheese off our plates in the lunchroom, for which we were awarded stickers on a big chart showing that we were part of the "Clean Plate Club." In the fifth grade we learned to march in PE as soldiers marched (to our great disappointment because we wanted to play basketball). And always there were guns: guns on war planes, guns on battleships, guns in foxholes, and at home, guns in cereal boxes, and in Christmas boxes under the tree.

After school and on Saturdays we fought the war in the pasture and behind the barn. We dug foxholes, crawled through the grass on our bellies, and climbed the tallest trees to scout the enemy. When we spotted the enemy we killed them. We didn't kill just a soldier or two. We killed squadrons and battalions and divisions. We shot them dead, several times over. Sometimes we were killed ourselves in return, or at least seriously wounded. We never simply fell over when shot. We clutched our chests, staggered around, made dramatic contortions of face, head, and legs, and swooned.

On other occasions we captured one another and made prisoners of war. We knew how prisoners were treated. They were humiliated. They were stripped to the waist, tied with hands behind their backs, and lashed. All that helped to take care of our sadistic tendencies.

Guns were an indispensable part of this. We didn't have to have store-bought guns; a stick or pointed finger would do. Boys with guns swaggered. Guns were power—over birds, over cans on the fence, over playmates, and over an enemy far away. It might be that today guns are used exclusively for sports, and as a hobby, with little symbolic significance beyond that, but back then, in the pasture and on the playground, in my hometown of LaGrange, guns were what you killed with. It was not unusual for a boy who had been teased or bullied to pull out his pretend gun and shoot someone.

Ours was a violent culture. That was not particularly surprising. We live in a fallen world. Much of our culture has always been violent, from the days of the frontier to the gang wars of the cities and in numerous wars the world over. And it evidenced itself even in the most innocent-appearing games.

Like Marbles. In lower elementary school we played marbles. We accumulated marbles. Marbles were wealth. We jiggled them in our pockets. Sometimes a boy would pull a handkerchief out of his pocket and a marble would fall out on the wooden floor in class. It sounded like a shot. The class tittered. The marble then belonged to the teacher.

The thrill of marbles was in the gaming. The games were called "pot" and "odd or even" or "shooters." If there were card sharks in the old west, there were marble sharks in LaGrange elementary school.

I don't know how old I was before I tried it. I watched for days. I practiced at home. Then I took several marbles and tested out the world. I jiggled the marbles in my pocket and walked over to where the action was. A boy named Ned asked if I wanted to play.

"Yeh"—I was careful not to appear too eager.

Ned was two years older than I was. He gave me first try. Aim your shooter at the marble. If you hit it you kept it. I missed. He shot, and hit, on his first try. He picked up my marble, put it in his pocket, and asked, "Want to try again?" It all happened in a period of fifteen seconds.

Nothing in the way I was raised to that point in my life had prepared me for the loss of that first marble. I had lost games before, but not games where part of me was taken for a prize. I'm not sure what I was expecting, but what I got was a rude awakening to the real world, where some are winners and some are losers and I was a loser.

"You want to play again?" He repeated the question.

I shook my head. There were tears in my eyes. I suppose that if the teacher had asked that day who would answer a question about letters in the alphabet, I would not have raised my hand.

It took several weeks before I tried again. Some things I learned from my mother, and some from my father. It was not a characteristic of my father's family to take defeat easily, or lightly. In my elementary school way, I schemed. See who is not very good and play against them. Pretend you are not as good as you are. If playing someone you thought you could beat, you offered a pretty marble to attract them into playing. If you played someone older or better than you, you offered a "chippie," or even a clay marble. The odds were against you, but you had little to lose. Marble hustling.

Whether I came out ahead or behind in the long haul, I do not remember. I do know there were some big winners. They were not only talented, but smart. Many played for big stakes, twenty or thirty marbles in a pot. Others lost big. Maybe they were born losers. They were gullible. They were not talented or smart, and others took advantage of that.

Such was the marble culture at our school. One way to peer standing was to win at marbles. But winning was always at someone else's expense. If there was a philosophical lesson it was Darwinism: survival of the fittest.

On the playground we made do without play equipment. I don't know if it was because we couldn't afford it, or because the educators thought that play equipment was dangerous. If it was the latter the educators didn't know how dangerous games without play equipment could be. One of our games was pom-pom-pull-away. Two lines, opposite each other. Someone in the center was "it." Kids ran from one line to the other. If they were tapped, they joined anyone in the center until all were caught. From time to time some yelled, "Pom-pom-pull-away!" and everyone had to run.

The game seemed simple enough, and sometimes when adults or teachers were around (they usually came around after someone had been hurt) it was played as described. But pom-pom-pull-away, along with its several variations, degenerated early and often on our schoolground. The bigger kids added a twist on the rules: not a single tap but three times on the back. The best way to tap someone three times was to catch them first, or actually, to tackle them, and that's when pom-pom-pull-away began to look suspiciously like tackle football played without a ball.

Crossing from one base to the other was like open-field running after the kickoff. Some kids resorted to quickness and end runs. Bigger boys bucked the line like fullbacks. Boys who could not be stopped one-on-one were gang tackled. Friends protected friends. Bigger boys looked out for smaller boys. Sometimes they crossed in groups with flying wedges. Otherwise, they straight-armed and hit low and knew all about the rolling block before they ever saw it in a football game.

It was controlled violence. It was a way to work off hostility. Grudges were settled and reputations established in pom-pom-pull-away. It was one of several games where courage and toughness were rewarded. Status among peers was determined in part by toughness on the playground.

What was not settled on the playground was settled after school.

The "bullies," particularly, restricted by teachers during school hours, evened their scores off the school grounds. They had scores to settle. Bullies usually were kids who were a grade or two, or even three, behind because they had flunked. They were teased and taunted unmercifully. What they accomplished at marbles or pom-pom-pull-away was offset by remarks about their being "dumb" or a titter when could not answer a question in class. Cruelty had many forms.

One either had to make peace with bullies (some kind of "pay-off" occasionally) or one had to know how to fight, or run. Sometimes we formed alliances and worked one bully against another. Sometimes we relied on different routes home from school. Some of us on the south side never went north to Lightning Hill because that's where the tough boys were.

All this—pretend guns and war games and marbles and pom-pom-pull-away—was part of growing up. I have no reason to believe the experience in my home town of LaGrange was appreciably different from the experiences of others of my generation in their schools. These experiences offered a school for life, for survival of the fittest and machismo in a competitive world. Boys I grew up with marched easily off to war, fought in barroom brawls, organized strikes, entered lawsuits, and schemed in the business world.

But growing up I was aware of an alternative world.

I never owned a gun. My mother did not like guns. I knew that instinctively. When I was five the neighbor boy, Jimmy, who was seven, came over loaded with holsters and pistols. Jimmy went to Saturday night movies and knew how cowboys shot people. He demonstrated. In fact, he demonstrated frequently. Any number of cowboys and Indians and Japs and dogs and neighbors walking by on the way uptown were leveled by Jimmy's fast six-shooter.

My mother was horrified. She never said as much, but it seemed that when Jimmy started blazing away with his pistols, it was always time for me to go in for lunch. I heard her talk to Father about "the neighborhood," and how maybe we should move.

Mother really didn't want guns around in any form, whether in pictures on the wall or out of cereal boxes. The birthday-present store-bought cowboy pistol disappeared. When I asked Mother one day why we didn't go to movies, she spoke about guns and killing and drinking, thus setting a standard for acceptability for movies that prevailed for several years. Mother was not against the war effort, but would have preferred to have fought it without guns. She liked the idea of cleaning up the macaroni and cheese and the clean-plate club—which we practiced at home in addition to school—as a way to win the war, but she was not fond of my being a part of the army that wiped out battalions of enemy soldiers in the pasture, an activity that for the most part was hidden from her.

Sometime, quite early in life, I made the connection between mother's view on guns and mother's hometown, Berne, Indiana. Mother's father lived in Berne, and her sisters and most of the eighty-three first cousins on her mother's side. The Church (it must always have been written with a capital C) was in Berne--the Mennonite church that is. Mother was a Mennonite. Her name was on the Methodist membership roll, but in her heart she was Mennonite, as were her sisters and cousins and everyone on the family tree as far back as it was recorded. And as were also most of the people of Berne—teachers at school, merchants who sold candy, and kids at the park. And on any given Sunday morning, and sometimes during the week, sixty percent of everyone in the whole town—thirteen hundred or so—could be found in the Mennonite Church. The other churches divided up the forty percent. The devil had to scrounge for anyone who somehow happened to fall through the cracks.

Mennonites didn't know anything. That's the way I had it figured at age nine. That is, they didn't know anything about the war. The children who came to play when I stayed with Aunt Selma did not bring guns and holsters and toy soldiers and bombers. They didn't know how to climb trees to scout the enemy, and blow up buildings with hand grenades, and be killed by clutching your chest, making contortions of the face, and swooning. They could not imagine capturing baby brothers and tying them up as prisoners of war.

I sometimes wondered if they even knew in Berne that there was a war. There were soldiers from Berne, but very few of them ever wore their uniforms when they walked down Main Street on furlough. None of the boys ever wore uniforms to church, there to be recognized and treated as heroes, as they were in Methodist churches. Homes did not hang little flags with stars on them in Berne windows, and no one sang, "Praise the Lord and Pass the Ammunition." There were no war memorials in the park in Berne.

Mennonites were pacifists. They did not believe in bearing arms and going to war to resolve conflict. The forefathers had been martyred for that conviction. Indeed, it was one reason why they were in America and not in Germany or Russia or England. And when they gathered the Mennonites spoke a great deal about Peace and Obedience and Suffering for Jesus' sake and the Sermon on the Mount. When I attended the Berne Bible school, which I did every year for five weeks in the summer, one of the very first passages of Scripture we memorized was the Beatitudes—*Blessed are the poor… Blessed are the meek…Blessed are the peacemakers…Blessed are you when you are persecuted.*

Mennonite pacifism was severely tested during World War II in Berne (it was worse in World War I but that is a different story). If there ever were a war behind which the country was united, and a cause which seemed just, it was the war against Hitler. And that meant agony in the decision facing Mennonite young men, how to reconcile loyalty to country with convictions passed down from generation to generation, for which their fathers in the faith had suffered, convictions about turning the other cheek and not killing and praying for enemies.

Mother and the relatives closest to us argued that "Peace" was not one of the essentials of the faith. Fundamentalism had crept into the Mennonite Church, and dispensationalism, and a skepticism about making the world better by not resisting evil. "Peace," they felt, should not be put on the same level with, say, the "blood of Jesus." Bearing arms should be a matter of individual conscience. The church ought to give support whether one bore arms, or served as a non-combatant, or did "alternate service", or sat in jail by conviction. It was, in modern terms, a "pro-choice" argument. Others did not agree. Such talk seemed a betrayal of the disciplined community and four hundred years of Anabaptist tradition.

The issue was always discussed with soft voices. Indeed, all things were discussed with soft voices in Berne, or at least it seemed so to a nine-year old. In my home town Fathers screamed at Mothers; Mothers screamed at children; and children screamed at other children, but in Berne, people spoke in soft voices.

And they did not fight. At least, they did not fight often. When boys fought, there was no glory in it. Fighting, and that associated with it—anger, verbal abuse, cursing—represented a tragedy to be discussed later with hushed voices. When mothers were told about some boy down the street who had been fighting, they would shake their heads and say, "What would his grandfather think?" Grandfathers, even dead ones, even other people's grandfathers, discouraged many a fight.

And since fighting wasn't popular in Berne, it was to be expected that pom-pom-pull-away would not be popular. My attempts to explain the game to friends at Berne met with polite silence. At about that time it occurred to me that Mennonite kids in Berne did not do the same things that kids in LaGrange did. Somehow in growing up, kids in Berne missed out on cowboys and Indians, war games, comic books, and movies. They were good at baseball, hop-scotch, hide-and-seek, and kick-the-can, but they never had the heart for marbles for "keeps," apple fights, or arguments in loud voices.

In my elementary school way, I tried to figure it out. It was because, I concluded, people in my hometown were Methodists, but in Berne they were Christians.

I have heard it argued, in more recent years, that those people who try to live quite literally by the Sermon on the Mount—Mennonites, for example—are not well fitted for the real world. The point is well made. Persons I knew from my mothers' home town did not easily march off to war, fight in barroom brawls, join strikes, enter lawsuits, or scheme in the business world. They were not good at arguing, screaming at one another, and beating their kids. So I suppose I agreed—they were not well fitted for the "real world."

But then, is Christianity itself meant to be well fitted for the "real world?"

I never owned a gun. Even yet. Perhaps especially yet. It is a conscious decision now, not just for me personally but also for my family. It is not so much about guns but about life itself, about the things that are important, and whose we are.

High School, La Grange, Ind.

The LaGrange School

Is it possible to be emotionally attached to a school building? Well, yes, I think it is, especially if it's the only school building you ever knew. Some kids move around and have to get used to different schools. They go to nursery school in one place, elementary school in another, middle school in another, and then high school in another. And that's assuming their parents aren't moving around from one city to another and dumping their kids in a new school system every time they move. How can you get to love a school building if you only spend two years in it?

I attended my LaGrange school twelve years, all in one building. It was grade school, junior high, and high school all rolled into one. We could root for our high school basketball team when we were third graders because we knew the players. We could see them in the rest rooms and in the hallways every day. The cheerleaders were like movie stars. I knew when the one-hand jump shot was introduced in

LaGrange because I saw Chuck Smith try it in the gym at the noon lunch break one day. We heard the coach tell him it wasn't a good shot. You had less control on the ball with one hand. Then Chuck made 9 out of 10 free throws one-handed. That settled it. Within a week every kid who could hold a basketball was trying the one-hand jump shot. We all learned together. We were like a big family.

I wasn't thinking family, however, when I entered the first grade in September, 1940. This was a new adventure. We first graders were scared about school. We didn't know what to expect. Could we get along without our mothers? Would we flunk? Would we get lost walking home? We didn't ease into it gradually, like kids today, who spend time in day care, then nursery school, then kindergarten. By the time they get to the first grade they've had four years of getting ready. None of us in my first grade had any getting ready time. We went directly from being home with mother to the care of the first grade teacher.

No wonder some kids cried when they got there. I didn't cry, but I did have concerns. Actually, one concern. I was worried about knowing where the rest rooms were, I was willing to try this thing called school but I didn't want to embarrass myself with, like an accident, and I was too shy to ask about a rest room, especially since I knew I was going to have a woman teacher. My friend, Duane Billman, assured me he knew where the rest rooms were and he would show me. But what if he wasn't there when I needed him?

Nothing to worry about. Mother took me to school, with tears, I think; I had no idea why. I could understand kids crying, but whey would mothers want to cry? They were getting rid of us. When the mothers finally left, our teacher, Miss Cobb, got right to the important business of the hour, namely, to show us where the rest rooms were. She was assisted by Mr. LeMaster. Mr. LeMaster was the superintendent of schools. That didn't impress me at all at the time; he might as well have been Ollie, the janitor. But years later I was impressed. We didn't have just anybody show us the rest rooms; we had the superintendent of schools. Miss Cobb took the girls. Mr. LeMaster took the boys.

Actually in those days we didn't call them rest rooms. They were toilets. The girls' toilets and the boys' toilets. We weren't refined yet. We first graders soon found out that Mr. LeMaster had another job; he did the paddling. The paddling room, which was really his office, was right next door to the first grade room. The door was always closed. As far as we knew the only thing that happened there was that kids got paddled. From time to time we heard loud cries coming from that room, and whacks; and if we happened to be in the hall, we could watch as kids would come out with tears streaming down their faces. In 1940 that had the marvelous effect of inspiring first graders to behave. Schools don't do that today, but kids today don't behave either. Rumor was Mr. LeMaster had a collection of those paddles, some with holes; the holes were supposed to hurt more. If there was ever a class of submissive first graders we were it.

But paddling and being submissive came later. First we had to know where the toilets were. So we lined up, and walked single file, out of our first grade room, past the second graders--presumably they already knew where the toilets were--down the hall, to the right, down a long flight of steps to a landing, turned left, down another flight of stairs, into the underground. Actually it was a big, dark room in the underground. Somewhere down there below sea level. There were no windows down there. It was scary.

Years later when I visited the Tower of London I had this feeling I had been there, or someplace like it, before. It is a famous prison, you know. Then I remembered: the boys' toilet at the LaGrange school.

There was a dim light bulb in this big underground room. I think if you were being grilled by the police, they would take you into a room like that. No pictures on the wall; no carpet; no friendly signs; it was grey and hard and uninviting.

Down at one end on one side of this dungeon-like room was the tin trough. Mr. LeMaster didn't need to explain what the trough was for. We were pretty smart first graders; at one end of the trough was a step. Mr. LeMaster didn't have to explain that either. You're little; you stand on the step. Some of the boys, all excited about this new adventure, had to try it out immediately. They lined up. And so, except for a small rest room under the gym, and one in the locker room, that trough serviced all the boys of the whole school, for 12 years, for 65 years before that, for 25 years after that; it was a very historic tin trough.

Even at that time I wondered, why such a big room for such a small trough? I don't know whether anybody else who attended school there ever wondered about that or not. The reason was, I found out later, that in the early years, before the gym was build, which was in the 1920s, not all that long before 1940, this big rest room, which reminded one of the Tower of London, was actually the gym. I don't know where they put the trough in those early days. Of course you couldn't play basketball in this gym; but when that school was built no one ever heard of basketball. According to one description in the 1870s, the new school boasted of a fine basement which was used for furnace purposes with rooms for storing wood (this building predated coal even), and other rooms for "exercising the scholars in inclement weather." Hah, I know what that meant— "exercising the scholars in inclement weather"--that spelled "gym." So the original school had a gym which later became a boys' toilet.

But I still had some anxieties. I knew what the trough was for, but sometimes, well, you needed more than that. No worry. They had thought of that too. Mr. LeMaster had to wait until all these boys had had their turns, then he took us up three steps and through a door to another room, even farther back in the underground catacombs. There was only one door into that room. Block that door and you would be stuck forever. In that room—which, if you didn't know it was there, you would never find it--were the indoor outhouses. I don't know what else to call them; that's what they were: communal indoor outhouses with stalls. There were long boards with holes in them separated by dividers. They were in one long row, which extended around the corner and along the back side. One stall had a door. That was the teachers' special outhouse. It took only a few days to realize we could look under the door to find out if any teachers were there.

This wasn't the arrangement we had at home, or even at church, but who was I to question it? This was school, and there weren't any other alternatives.

There were problems. The seats were high, at least for first graders. You had to crawl up or scoot up, trying to take care of your pants which were inconveniently situated because of the occasion. And so you sat there, with your feet dangling, trying to balance, feeling insecure. And then just when you thought you could make it, and everything was going to be OK, there was terror to strike fear into the heart of every little boy. I later called it the Big Flush. It would start with some noise from far away like a train coming into town from Lima, getting closer and closer, and if you didn't know what it was, you thought the whole school was going to be swept away. It was a tsunami, I didn't know that word in the first grade but that's what it was. A tidal wave.

What was that all about? Well, I figured that out on my own. They had this big water tower down by the library and the Lutheran Church. And on top of that water town, up in the big tank, there was water, lots of water, a whole lake of water. Before, I had wondered why that was there; now I knew. Every so often, maybe after the fourth graders had been in there, someone was responsible for turning some big valve. I mean it had to be big. And the pipe in the middle of that tower was, how big? Ten feet across--and they opened that valve, and the water came roaring down, all the way to the school, through secret passages and huge pipes, until it reached the underground outhouses, and whatever was down there, down in that dark part under the holes, was swept away.

Eventually I figured out where it went. Down to Fly Creek. And if you knew where it entered Fly Creek, you could probably find all kinds of stuff, stuff that had gotten flushed away: mittens, ball gloves, arithmetic papers, pencils. If you lost something you could run down there to retrieve it. Otherwise it was gone, to the Pigeon River, to the St. Joe, to Lake Michigan, Ste. St. Marie, Lake Huron, Lake Erie, Niagra Falls, Lake Ontario, St. Lawrence Seaway, and the Atlantic Ocean. "What happened to your arithmetic paper?" "Hey, it got sucked in by the Big Flush and it's out in the Atlantic Ocean."

I kind of had the idea that school building had been there for 100 years, or back to the beginning of the town. Maybe the Indians built it. Not so; there was a school that predated it. One school went broke, that was before public schools; you had to pay to go to that school. When it failed the building was bought by the Methodist

Church. Another school was too small and was purchased in 1866 by the Moon brothers who moved it to the south side of town and used it in the carriage and wagon manufactory. I remember the building. It wasn't too far from the town dump.

But LaGrange was coming up in the world, with illusions of grandeur. Those early dreamers were going to outdo anyone else around and so in 1874, the forefathers built this huge brick structure, a prestige-enhancer, big enough to care for 480 students. It cost $30,000, which was a lot then. The town paper announced with pride that LaGrange had a graded school. A graded school is no big thing now, but then it was. Before that time schools did not have grades. You just learned at your own level until you knew as much as the teacher and you quit.

By 1880 the LaGrange school enrolled 300 students, which was not a whole lot fewer than they had in 1940. I had a great-aunt Gay that lived out in the hinterlands, out by Woodruff. Her parents, my great-grandparents, sent her into town; she probably stayed with some relatives so she could attend the graded school and get a degree from the prestigious LaGrange High School. I found a program of her graduation exercises. It was nicely printed honoring ten graduates in the class of 1891. On the program was a picture of the school, and it looked exactly like the school I attended in 1940.

The school added a gymnasium sometime in the 1920s. Before that basketball games were played in the old (abandoned) Free Will Baptist Church which stood at the head of Hawpatch Road in the middle of the county. The Baptists didn't make it, so the building reinvented itself as a gym and after that it reinvented itself again as a body shop. Serves the Baptists right, moving in on the Methodists in LaGrange.

The descriptions of the school of those early times spoke of three stories plus the basement with the rooms for wood and the tin trough and the indoor outhouses and the gym. Plus the tower for the offices. I often thought those tower rooms would be a great place for an office. There were windows on three sides. You could look out and see who was coming and going. Kids skip school you could open the window and yell at them.

The third floor was where the assembly was. One big room. But nobody went up there in my time. When they added the new gym in the 1920s they also added an assembly room and closed off the third floor. If anyone ever went up there I don't know how they did it. They had taken out the stairs. Later I wondered how they ever kept the pigeons out. It must have been a pigeon heaven. Thus the third floor became a mystery. Maybe there were bodies there. Maybe some kid was told to stand in the corner and he is still there, that is, his bones. If someone wanted to do something illegal, like counterfeit money, or start a moonshine operation, that would be the place to do it.

I asked someone once why they closed it off.

"It's not safe."

That hardly resolved the mystery. Why was it not safe? Was the floor rotting? Was the ceiling caving in? If so maybe everything would someday come crashing through the second floor ceiling into the world history room.

That would be fairly dramatic.

I suspect now it was not safe because of possible fire. One misshap and that building, which was all wood, would make a fireball that could be seen in all LaGrange County. Presumably you could jump out of a second story window, in case of a fire. You might break a leg or something but you would be alive. The third floor was a different story. You would be smashed into a big blob.

When I went to Berne to Bible school for five weeks each summer I became acquainted with another type of school. The Berne school (where Bible school was held) was a brand new school. But it was boring. True, the rest rooms had real toilets, but by that time I had come to like our trough. At Berne the rooms were all the same with modern desks and cement floors with some kind of covering.

At my school all the desks were wooden with names carved on them. Scholars of the past were memorialized with their names, or at least their initials. Sometimes they even carved the year. Some kid had used that desk in 1932. We were threatened with death if we had any thoughts of carving our names on the desks in the 1940s.

Besides the wooden desks we had wooden floors, beautiful

varnished wooden floors. You could smell varnish all the time; if I had to describe the smell of the school it would be like varnish. But that was a nice, clean smell. Ollie the janitor used a lot of varnish. People today would pay good money for the wood that was on those floors. The floors made noise. Wonderful, loud, disrupting noise, unsoftened by curtains or carpet. And with all the wood there were marvelous echoes. If you were the only one in the school you could call out your name and it would echo upstairs and down and through the halls. And when you would clump down the stairs you could make noises like rolling thunder. And the guys, maybe the girls too, made the most of it. Drag your feet down the stairs and it sounded like a train, especially if you were wearing clodhoppers. Clodhoppers were the big heavy boots the country kids wore. My mother never let me get a pair. I felt deprived. The heavier the boots the more noise you could make going up and down the stairs. However, when they started giving dancing lessons some of us got taps on our shoes. Then we could compete with the clodhoppers.

What I remember is: the bell would ring. Kids would stream out of classes and head for the stairs to drag their feet or tap their taps just to see how much noise they could make; there was this mighty roar for 5 minutes, then we would start the next class and it would be quiet for another hour.

Miss Cobb was a good teacher, there in the first grade. I always thought she should get married so she wouldn't have a name like Cobb any more. No one called her Miss Cobb behind her back; she was always Corn Cob. Unlike other teachers I don't think she was originally from LaGrange; usually we got our teachers locally. She did her thing at LaGrange and then moved to Decatur. I always thought that was sad, to leave all the students you had taught to go to some lesser place like Decatur, Indiana. Years later I was preaching someplace in Michigan and at the fellowship time after the service someone said to me, your first grade teacher is here. Sure enough it was Miss Cobb. When I knew her in the first grade she was 6 feet tall, or so it seemed, and beautiful and smiled a lot. Fifty-five years later she was four feet tall and stooped and old. But it was good to see her. She remembered me.

I sat in the third seat in the third row in the first grade. Miss Cobb used flash cards to teach us letters and words. I remember mostly, however, her teaching us to write. Script, with wonderful swirls. Capital letter Q's like no one ever makes anymore. Occasionally students got disciplined. For doing something or other they had to sit in the corner. I felt so sorry for those students, mostly boys but occasionally girls. But we were generally well behaved. We were not the ones that screamed from the paddle room next door. Those were mostly fifth and sixth graders.

That disciplining was not unrelated to another of my first grade experiences, namely, a crush on a third-grade girl. I have not the slightest idea why a first grade boy would get a crush on a third-grade girl; but I did. It was a crush from afar, sort of like Charlie Brown and the little red-headed girl. I would die if I ever had to speak with her, and as far as I know I never did. My crush consisted mostly of watching for her either on the playground or whenever the third graders came filing by. I also fantasized. You say, what do first grade boys think about when they fantasize about third grade girls? Well, it had to do with sitting in the corner. I would day dream about her being disciplined for something she did not do and I would be superman. I knew superman from comics. I would come rushing in and rescue her from humiliation, from a mean teacher, from the closet or the corner, and take her to safety.

By the time I got to the second grade I developed a crush on someone a bit more appropriate--Ann Paulen. The preacher's daughter, Ann Paulen, was one grade behind me, in the first grade. I did know her; I played with her, even stayed overnight at her house. The attraction there was her red hair. Years later I had a sort-of date with her. At least I went for a walk with her around Epworth Forest, our church camp, and when you are teen-ager keeping score, a walk around church camp at night qualifies as a date.

Our school had no playground equipment. We had recess in a big lot, or a field. There were no swings, no teeter-totters, and no merry-go-rounds. I am not exactly sure why, but I think someone thought we could get hurt on things like that. So we played "safe" games, like pom-pom-pullaway and Red Rover. Those games actually were as dangerous as any playground games that could be devised, especially the way we played them. In Red Rover everyone held hands and someone ran from the other side and tried to break through the line. The object of the game was to knock as many people down as you could.

We also played softball work-up. Some of the boys in the fifth and sixth grades were pretty good. For some of the bigger boys the goal was to break a window. It seemed an unattainable goal but one day it happened. The first grade window. I think it was Ottie Stewart. A big swing, a solid hit, a long fly, and a dramatic smash. Right into the first-grade room. The kids cheered. After that the ball diamond was moved.

By the second grade some of the first grade inhibitions were gone. We moved one room to the right. We were still close enough to the superintendent's office to hear the paddling. I remember the day when some of the boys in our class were reported for snowballing. We weren't supposed to throw snowballs at school. There might be stones in the snowball and we could put out an eye. We had been warned; but some of the class got carried away and there was a snowball fight. No eyes were put out but it didn't matter. Mr. LeMaster was very busy that day. They called out the boys one by one. It was a solemn occasion. Boys came back rubbing their behinds and wiping their eyes.

Mr. LeMaster was also responsible for saving the town of LaGrange from the breakdown of society that comes with inappropriate observances of Halloween. I don't know if it was his idea mainly or the school board's or the town council's. At any rate, sometime around the first of November we got a day off school if we had not committed any vandalism at Halloween. Vandalism was defined as trick or treating, soaping windows or upsetting outhouses. As if we in the second grade were going to upset outhouses. Frankly, I couldn't think of anything more revolting. But if we didn't do it we got a day off school. Kids who got reported sat all day in assembly hall with some poor teacher who I hope was being paid for being there. I don't know of any other town in the world which prohibited trick or treating during Halloween, but LaGrange did.

By the second grade, or maybe the third, we all did our part to win World War II. This consisted mostly of eating all the macaroni and cheese on our plates in the lunch room. I never was sure how this was going to win the war, but, hey, who was I to question the wisdom of the teachers? Eat the macaroni and win the war. So I ate it. It would have helped if the macaroni and cheese were good, but it wasn't. It was mostly dry macaroni with not much cheese. I haven't liked macaroni and cheese much ever since. Some kids, as I recall, cheated. They secretly scraped their plates while the teacher wasn't looking. Now we were never going to win the war. I would have tattled more—some of the other kids did, mostly the girls—but I could hardly blame them. The food was awful tasting. For our efforts we got a little sticker to paste on a poster. We were part of the clean-plate club. I thought we should receive the medal of honor or something for getting all stickers on the poster, but we didn't. I guess it was enough to win the war because eventually we won it.

We also sang war songs, (propaganda songs actually), to help win the war. They were patriotic songs full of references to freedom and liberty and good old America and the boys overseas and fighting the "Japs."

The louder we sang the quicker the war would be over. After we sang the songs we walked in a long line down to the post office to spend our dimes for a stamp to put in our war bond stamp book. A kid needed $18.75 to fill a book and get a bond. At 10 cents a crack that meant it would take 188 trips to the post office. If there were 180 days in the school year, it meant a kid could not fill up a book in a whole year, and that's assuming he walked down there every day school was open. But who were we to ask questions? If it would win the war, we would take the walk.

In the third grade our teacher was Ocie Marker. She liked us so well she came back in 7th grade. By that time she was Ocie Olds. Then, if that weren't enough, she had us for the 8th grade. I might even have handled that but then she also was my Sunday school teacher for three more years. She didn't have to send kids to the superintendent's office to have them whacked with a paddle with holes in it. I recall she could do that all by herself. We could have her sent to jail today for corporal punishment the way she whacked those seventh grade boys. I don't think she ever did it in Sunday school. Today kids don't get wacked, but they don't behave too well either.

We honored Ocie in the third grade with fruit rolls. Sometimes because we loved them or because it was their birthday, or for no reason at all, we organized fruit rolls for our teachers. This was a great LaGrange custom that never caught on worldwide. On a designated day all the kids would bring fruit from home. Apples and oranges worked best, though a pear or a tomato or a grapefruit was acceptable. Even melons would work. There were problems with bananas because they did not roll well. We asked the teacher to read a story and then, half-way through the story, at a given signal we all rolled the fruit up front and cried out, "Fruit roll!" The teacher would then take the bounty home, wash it off, feed it to her kids if it weren't too beat up, and know that we all loved her.

Or "him." When we made it to the 5th and 6th grades, we had men teachers, Mr. Kilpatrick and Mr. Plasterer. We gave them fruit rolls too, even mean Mr. Kilpatrick. We didn't like Mr. Kilpatrick much because he made us march in gym class, like we were in the army reserve or something. We wanted to play basketball. But it was war time and he believed we needed to know how to march.

It was when I was in the fifth grade with Mr. Kilpatrick that the fruit rolls ceased. The class ahead of us, the class of '51, spoiled it not only for us but for all future generations of kids at LaGrange school. In one ten-second display of grade-school havoc they wiped out years of fruit roll tradition. What happened is that instead of a gentle fruit-roll some of the boys stood up and threw over-ripe tomatoes at the teacher. I don't know if Mr. LeMaster got his paddles with holes in them out for that one or not. I do know that that was fruit rolls were banned from then on for all times in all places and for all reasons.

We had other interesting customs at LaGrange. For grades we did not get A's, or B's, or C's like everyone else in Indiana, or in the world. We got 1's, 2's, 3's, all the way up to 6's. If we were talking to someone from another school and they asked what kind of grades we got, we could say, 2's, 3's, 5's, or 6's. What in the world is that? If we were good at arithmetic (no one called it math then) we would explain 1 was for 96%-100%, 2 for 91%-95%, and all the way down. Theoretically a kid could get a grade of 19 for 5% on his or her paper, but the school was merciful. Kids never got lower than a 6.

Finally, most of us (a few kids kept repeating the 6th grade) finished grade school and got promoted to upstairs and junior high. We moved up about the same time World War II was over. It was a new day. There were new worlds to conquer. But we were ready. We were the big kids now.

711 Hawpatch

In 1940—I was six years old at the time--my family moved to 711 Hawpatch in LaGrange, Indiana. My father bought the house and the property for $5,000. I think that was a lot in 1940. What he got for $5,000 was a big old house and a whole city block-- actually two city blocks--except for one corner where the Pierces lived. These

711 Hawpatch, LaGrange, Indiana, 1940s

were really town blocks, not city blocks, but city blocks sounds more impressive. I never have known how big it was for sure, but I think we used to say five acres. This was not five acres on the outskirts of town, but five acres in the middle of town. Well, not really in the middle, more on the south side; there were two streets laid out farther south than our street.

LaGrange had been around for about 100 years at the time. It was the county seat. That has a special significance in Indiana. It meant doctors and lawyers and judges and the court house. We had a famous courthouse—still do—built by someone well-known in 1872 or so, a great courthouse square with maple trees. LaGrange was a shopping center for a whole area, at least at that time. Its rivals for shopping were Elkhart, 30 miles west; Sturgis, Michigan, 12 miles north; Angola, 22 miles east; or Kendallville 20 miles south. To the little towns around we were the big city. They delighted to beat us in basketball. They were delighted a lot since they beat us regularly.

The population was about 1,800 and hadn't varied much before or after.

LaGrange, in 1940, was made up of:

1) The north side, north of U.S. 20 and west of Detroit Street. The north side was settled first. Important people lived there. The original founders lived there, in big brick houses which were featured in the several city and county histories and in old postcards. The prestigious streets were Michigan Street and Spring Street.

2) The east side, east of Detroit St. and mostly across the tracks. There was a different class of people there. If you grow up class conscious, and small towns are more class conscious even than cities I believe, across the tracks meant lower class. Of course I didn't think in terms of class growing up. But even I was aware that Methodists tended not to live over there. That's where my paper route was, by the way. I could identify with folks there. I loved those people, but it was not the same as our part of town.

3) The south side, or everything south of U.S. 20. The prestigious street on the south side was Hawpatch Street. Sometimes it was Hawpatch Road. It was a street until you hit the city limits; then it became road. Hawpatch Street, in comparison to the lesser streets, had curbs. Only important streets had curbs. Many streets in our town in 1940 were still gravel. We not only were blacktopped; we had curbs all the way past our house. Two blocks south of our house the curbs stopped. That's where the prestige stopped.

Hawpatch was (and still is today) the only street in town that does not run straight east and west or north and south. It was an

Indian trail and it angles southwest, not only from the center of town but from the center of the county, the center being the junction of U.S. 20 and state road 9. Beyond our house, Hawpatch Road angled and curved and went up and down and around hills and swamps, to an area farther out which originally was called simply "the Hawpatch," so named because it was once a kind of no-man's land of tangled vegetation and lots of hawthorn trees (or shrubs). It was made famous because in early years horse thieves hid out there.

When people from the quarter of the county south and west of LaGrange came to "town" ("town" being LaGrange), they traveled Hawpatch Road. Since many of the people in that quarter of the county were Amish we could heard the clip-clop of horses' hooves day and night which, to people visiting us, added to the charm of the place, when it wasn't keeping them awake at night.

When the Amish came to LaGrange County in the 1850s or so they cleaned up the Hawpatch; they tiled the swamp, cleared the underbrush, and farmed the muck. Muck is the stuff left when the swamps are drained. It is so full of humus it will catch fire. The Amish grow marvelous crops there and get rich, at least by Amish standards. But they are humble and don't admit that they are rich.

There are lots of Amish in LaGrange County, so many that our county ranks #1 in Indiana as the county with the highest percentage of homes that do not use English as the first language. The Amish affect our statistics in other ways. LaGrange County is sometimes considered a poor county because of the number of homes without electricity and running water. It does not matter how much money is stuffed under the mattress; no electricity means the housing values are not as great and if houses are considered unimproved it looks on paper like people are poor there.

In the middle of the Depression, in 1937 my father was offered the job as County Extension Agent in LaGrange. The County Extension Agent was a big job then. Ours was a rural economy (some industry would come later) and almost everything was farming or farm related. This means if you were an expert on farming, which my father was supposed to be, you were important. My father had an office, a big room actually in a store front across the street south from the court house (he later moved to the basement of the post office). What I remember about the original office is all the pamphlets which hung on hooks on the wall, telling you anything you ever wanted to know about farming. If you were interested in such things, you could learn about pig diseases and pruning apples and how to raise chickens and what to do with horse manure. Next door to his office was the dentist I went to who took care of teeth without novocain.

We lived for a while on Poplar Street in a rented house. Then, in 1940 we moved to 711 Hawpatch. When we moved there it was 709 Hawpatch. One day, 20 years later, the postmaster told my father they had made a mistake when they gave us our street number. It was really not 709 but 711. It didn't matter. People didn't find our house by the street number. They just looked for the big trees and there we were.

711 Hawpatch wasn't a farm but it was the nearest thing to it. My mother never would have stood to live in the country. She was a city girl, if Berne, Indiana can be called a city. So Mother and Father had this compromise. We would live on what we pretended to be a farm in the middle of the city. It worked great. My father was only eight blocks from his office. On the five acres were a hill, a big pasture, a barn with three horse stalls, a big orchard, a big garden, chicken coops (plural), huge grape arbors (plural), cherry trees, apricots, pecan trees, gooseberries, apples, plums, and a swing tied to a limb 20 feet in the air. The swing was just one of many attractions for children, grandchildren, and neighborhood kids.

People would ask me if I grew up on a farm. I could sometimes answer yes, and sometimes no, depending on what kind of image I wanted to project. My father, I think, wanted it to be a farm for my sake. I think he thought I needed the farm experience. So during the course of several years Father brought in cows (actually, two cows which we kept not more than a year). I can't think he did that just because he loved cows; he wanted me to have the experience of milking cows. It worked. When I would date the girls I could say, "Yah, I used to milk cows by hand, back there in elementary school." That only impressed the 4-H type girls. The city girls never were impressed by farm images.

We also had horses and orphan sheep. The sheep ran loose like dogs until one wandered across the street and ate the neighbor's expensive roses; then we curtailed our sheep operation. Sheep were never made, let me tell you—and this is Biblical--to run free like dogs. Our sheep were slow learners. Of course that worked to advantage also as my sheep knowledge made it into numerous sermons in years after.

And of course we always had chickens. As soon as we moved we launched our chicken project. We had chickens over on Poplar Street--12 chickens in a big dog house-- but now we were going to go big time. This was my father's idea to teach me responsibility and to give me a love for farm things. Taking care of the chickens would substitute for an allowance and would be my specialty in 4-H. We tried the chickens in the coops. Actually they weren't coops but old houses that for some reason or other were on the property. Our first coop was too near the house for Mother so after a couple years we moved the one coop to another foundation, dug up the original chicken yard for a garden--great thinking on the part of my father since our garden now had a natural chicken fertilizer base--put another coop in the orchard and had chicks and broilers and laying hens all at the same time. We tried Leghorns and Barred Rocks and New Hampshire Reds and I don't know what all.

Like all farm chickens at that time our chickens ran more or less loose, which is what the environmentalists want these days, no chickens penned up. Chickens, we are being told presently, need freedom to run loose the way God intended, wandering throughout the neighborhood just like sheep once wandered around Judea. This meant the chickens ate grass and kitchen scraps, which made the yokes green which scared some people because they thought real eggs came only with yellow yokes.

People today don't know what green yokes are. But ours was environmentally advanced thinking before we knew it was fashionable. From time to time our chickens got hit by cars. If Dad could save a chicken hit by a car he would. This meant chop the chicken's head off immediately, pluck it and eat it. No use wasting a good chicken just because it got hit by a car. I remember the day--I was pretty young--after my father had done one of these, that he told me, "Now after this, if I'm not home that's your job."Sure enough, not long after that, it happened. A chicken got hit by a car and was flopping around. My mother was distraught, nearly hysterical actually. My sisters were hysterical. I did the job of a man. I chased the chicken down, got the ax, put the chicken's head on the block, whacked it off with one blow, and felt like Rambo. We ate the chicken that night. I did my father proud.

Eventually we moved the chicken operation to the second floor of the barn. I did the chicken thing for 10 years in 4-H. I filled out all the records, made a scrapbook as my father instructed, became a national 4-H poultry champion and got a small college scholarship. I've always been kind of embarrassed about that, for the chicken business was changing, and we still operated the old style way and I really wasn't much of an expert. But I made a name for myself and got my picture in the paper.

One day as a senior I brought chickens to school and in speech class gave a demonstration on how to cull a hen. You look at the comb, feel the hen back in the rear, where the eggs come out, to see if the bones are spread out meaning eggs are coming through. I pointed out the value of the chickens I had brought to school and offered to pass them around. "This one is good." "This one is ready for the pot." The girls were impressed. The teacher, who was actually the neighbor Mr. Pierce who lived next door, thought I was a show-off.

Along with chickens we did gardening. That was another 4-H project. The old chicken yard did well, as did another area that may at one time have been a cow pen. We grew stuff people don't like to eat today: kohlrabi, eggplant, parsnips, mustard greens, swiss chard, okra. I rather delighted in finding stuff no one else was growing and trying it out. This was especially true when my friend Raymond and I discovered we could exhibit in the open class at the Corn School and win prize money. Corn School at that time was like our county fair. And if you were the only one exhibiting parsnips--and frankly not too many people exhibited parsnips--you were sure to get a prize. Of course if you grew it you had to eat it. After I pretended to like it I was able, in years to come, to try anything.

In addition to what I picked out my father wanted to try some stuff, most of which he got from Purdue: purple peas and red cabbage and square tomatoes. Purdue wanted to develop square tomatoes with thick skins that would pack well when shipped. So we planted some. They worked. The tomatoes were more or less square. The only problem was that they tasted more like cardboard than tomatoes.

One day my father told me about the new thing: multi-flora rose. It was a shrub with pretty flowers that was good for wildlife and could function as a fence. We planted a long row along one side of the field. Dad soon discovered that not everything that Purdue suggests is for the betterment of humankind. That new development ranks along with the introduction of English Sparrows or Starlings in America as a great national disaster. It illustrates the Law of Unintended Consequences. It is recorded in books now as a classic example of the word "invasive." Today when I fight multi-flora rose on my property I think of the Purdue recommendation and sing the Indiana University fight song.

We tried other things. Father thought if he were recommending this stuff to other people we should have it at our own house. One of them was a sort of small-time root cellar; you take a big drainage tile, sink it about three feet in the ground, put down gravel and then leaves or saw dust or whatever, throw in your apples or turnips or potatoes or parsnips or carrots, and they're good until next summer. It works fine unless you are the kid who in the middle of January has to go out in the snow, take the cover off, crawl in head first three feet down, root around and come up with potatoes when you're looking for parsnips. And this you had to do even if you didn't like either carrots or parsnips.

I don't ever remember spraying anything. We fought weeds the old fashioned way, with a hoe and various whackers. We were organic before it was fashionable. Out in the pasture it was my job every so often to take a corn cutter and take out ragweed, burdock and thistles. There were big bumble bees out there that didn't like their bull thistles getting cut down. I was just a little kid. I was intimidated by the bumble bees. The upside was, I could pretend the corn cutter was a weapon and we were in the midst of World War II and every thistle was an enemy soldier. And so cutting thistles became a game.

Our lawn, if you called it a lawn--we called it a yard--was huge, not by today's standards but by standards established in the day before power mowers. Our lawn mower was human-powered. I was the power. I never could mow the yard in one day. I used a sermon illustration once when I was 55 years old about dreaming of this intimidating yard with quack grass. The yard with quack grass was like evil. It was always pressing in on all sides. My father was there. On the way home from church he apologized to me. He was sorry he made me work so hard. This 87-year old man apologizing to his 55-year old son. Then I had to apologize to him. "It's OK Dad, sometimes preachers exaggerate." Those are preacher-enhanced stories. Preachers need interesting childhoods if they are going to come up with sermon illustrations.

One day Wallace Billman, our neighbor and an uptown businessman, came over with a new thing, a rotary mower with an engine. He was the first dealer in town to handle rotary power mowers, the kind everyone has today. He started the mower up and mowed a swath through that quack grass. I don't think I was ever as impressed by any invention in the last 70 years. Television, rocket ships, computers, cell phones—none of them made an impact like that first power rotary lawn mower. My father bought one. The problem was when we got it my father figured we could now increase the size of our "yard."So we took a hunk out of the pasture for additional yard. So now I was mowing a field.

We had good neighbors. We had our share of important people, just like the folks on the north side of town. We were, after all, on Hawpatch Street, which was paved and had curbs. Some of our homes were pictured in the county history, just like the homes up on Michigan Street. Across the street and south the Billmans lived (Methodists)--Duane, my friend, and Emily, younger. Next to them and across the street were the Gohl's (Methodists)--Miriam and Lorna Kay. Lorna Kay was my sister's friend. Next to them lived the Norrises (Methodists), and their girls Romona and Eleanor.

When I was in the second grade I got stuck in the chicken coop with Eleanor. She was a first grader. Some things you don't forget. I had dragged her into that chicken coop to impress her and then had to tell her I couldn't get the door open to get out. Even as a second grader I didn't think it would set well with Mrs. Norris to find out her daughter had spent the night with a boy in the chicken coop.

Next to the Norrises were the Minnicks (Presbyterian)--Chuck my friend, and Shirley and Sharon, my sisters' friends. Down the street on that side were the Bachman's (Methodists)--Raymond my close friend, and Deanna, my sisters' friend. Across the street from them the Funks (Lutherans)--Lora Lee a year behind me in school, and Billy a couple of years younger. And, next door to our north, claiming a corner of our block, the Pierces (Presbyterian) with Jack and Jim and later, Carson Zimmerman, who had come to live with them. The kids were the core of the Hawpatch gang. They hung around our house a lot. We staked out a ball field in the front yard, under the trees.

Even when we first moved, when I had just started the first grade, I realized this was no ordinary property. There were, like, mysteries. For example, the grown-over sidewalks. On three sides of our property there were sidewalks, almost buried with weeds and grass and dirt. They were mostly slate sidewalks that obviously had not been used for years. On the long side of the property people walked on the road, not on the buried slate sidewalks. Why would people put sidewalks where no one ever walked? What was this place like, this town like, 50 years before, or 100 years, or who knows how many? Was this neighborhood once thriving with people? Ordinary homes don't have a half mile of sidewalks that had not been used for years.

Then there were the eight-foot fence posts. That was explained to us. Some owner in the past had kept reindeer. Reindeer? Of course they weren't real reindeer, which really don't exist, except on Santa's sleigh, or maybe in Lapland. These deer must have been plain old white-tails, but that did not take the mystery away. Deer in those days were not nearly as common as today. We never saw deer in the wild in our county. But evidently they could be seen at 711 Hawpatch, which was, at that time, 709 Hawpatch.

There were foundations of several long-gone out-buildings. What were those used for? They must have been sheds and cribs and mini-barns. One was evidently the main barn, a two story barn, probably originally a livery barn, with three stalls for horses, and a second floor for hay. In 1940 it was full of junk. Lots and lots of junk. We had moved in on top of someone else's left-overs. The junk was in the barn, in the chicken coops, in the two back rooms. Somebody, and maybe several somebodies, had simply left what they didn't want. And we inherited it all. All of this I knew predated Dr. Schultz, who lived there just before us, who had actually rented, and migrated from this place--probably couldn't handle it--to a big house on Michigan Street where the important people lived. He was an import, that is, he had not grown up in LaGrange. No family or history. He had lilly-white hands; not an appropriate hands for a farm in the middle of town. He had no interest in the orchard or chickens or the barn or the fences suitable for deer or the buried sidewalks. I don't know how long he was there but he eventually found a house on Michigan street more to his liking.

711 Hawpatch in 1940 had obviously been remodeled and resized and reformed a number of times. Bathrooms had been put in where there were none and stairs taken out where they were and put in where they weren't; there was a big slab of cement that we called the back porch but which was perhaps once a room. There were stairwells that weren't used. Entryways that were boarded up. The net result was what might best be described as a comglobulated mess. Rooms too small, especially the kitchen, the upstairs so arranged that all upstairs traffic had to move through my parents' bedroom to get to any other bedroom. This was very bad if you were a teen-ager trying to sneak in late.

And there were almost no closets. My father had to pass through my bedroom to get to his and my closet, which was actually an old stairwell. It was a long, narrow stairwell-closet that that went on and on and on. At the back, if you could fight through the clothes to get there, was storage place and an ideal spot to hide when we played hide-and-seek.

My mother could not walk into her closet and had to dress and undress in front of all her children or whoever the guests might be. When we moved there was a beautiful marble sink with antique fixtures in one room that was free standing and seemed unrelated to anything around it. I wish I had that now. On the back of the house were two rooms that seemed to have no practical purpose. I believe now one was a summer kitchen, common in fancy homes of the 1850s, 60s, and 70s. Or maybe it was a year-around kitchen (there were cupboards build in) and beyond that there was another room with a cistern in the floor—I have no idea what that was about—that may have been used for a shop. This cistern was in addition to another cistern in the basement. My father had the back-back room made into a garage. A little time snooping around that house, and one could believe in ghosts. It was like the spirits of those who had lived there before were still there.

But 711 Hawpatch was my house, with all of its quirks and idiosyncrasies. For years when I would come home I would walk around the property and check things out. I belonged there. Ruth did not feel the same way. After my father died I had a brilliant thought that we could keep that house until I retired and then we could live there. In fact I even suggested we could get appointed to the LaGrange Church and live in our own house and mentioned that to the district superintendent. Sometime later they called me up and offered me the church. It was a very short-lived brilliant thought that lasted only as long as it took to share with Ruth, who said something like: "I would never live there; in fact, I don't know who else in the world would ever live there if they had a choice except your parents." So that wasn't going to work.

Later in life I did research. I read all the histories. I went to the library and read the old newspapers on microfilm. I wanted to find out about Methodists, revivals, my relatives, and if possible, our house and the people who lived there. The house dated from 1870s; there was a reference to it in 1872. The abstract dated it somewhere there. It was built by a man named Rose who ran a dry goods store. He must have used the whole two blocks; an 1880 plat book shows a big orchard at the back of the property which would explain why there was a very old gnarled apple tree and a very gnarled old plum tree when we moved. It was left over from the 1870s orchard. I found one reference to the fine family of 10 children the Roses raised in their grove on Hawpatch.

The reference to the grove and the date immediately identified the age of the trees. People who spoke of our house would refer to it as the place with the big trees. I don't know how many trees make a grove but some were gone by 1940, and others left us during our 50 years there, including one that toppled over in a storm and just about wiped out my sisters' bedroom in 1942. Even after that there were 13 of the big trees left. There were some others but the 13 were in a different class. They were the patriarchs. They would have been 70 years old in 1940; they would be 135 years old today. Norway Spruce, Red Oak, Sugar Maple.

I broke my arm on second base in 1943. I was by myself and had hit a single for the St. Louis Cardinals in the World Series. When you play by yourself you do everything. You play offense and defense and announce the games and steal bases. Great fun. I had hit a long single and wanted to stretch it into a double and went head first into a 70 year old Red Oak second base. That was a little hard to explain. How did you break your arm? I was Stan Musial in the world series sliding head first into a 70 year-old Red Oak. Of course I didn't know at that time it was 70 years old; I just knew all those trees were big.

I knew every one of those trees. I had mowed around them and played around them for years. I knew how the roots curved around, where some hollow places were, where you could put your hand in a scoop out sawdust and ants. A few years after we sold the house, in the mid 1990s one of the trees came down and took out the 2nd floor room we called the guest room. It was dramatic enough that there were pictures in the paper.

After the Roses, the next family of note that raised a family in our house was Dr. Wade. Wade was a prominent LaGrange name. Raymond Wade, another Wade, who became a Methodist bishop, was from LaGrange. Dr. Wade must have been one of his relatives. Dr. Wade was a physician and his years were the 1910s, 20s, and 30s. Wade probably did most of the wacky things. Like the deer. And like the quince trees and the pecan trees and the asparagus patches and the grape arbors. There were four long rows of grapes, enough to make wine for the whole town. Father tore out three rows when we moved.

And Dr Wade must have done the second orchard. I would also assume that most of the junk in the barn, and behind the barn, and in the back rooms, was originally his.

The junk was enough to keep Duane, Raymond and me occupied for the better part of several years when I was in grade school. It really wasn't my thing but Duane Billman, my friend, was fascinated. He was a born mechanic and tinkerer. He tried to figure out what things were for, and he tried to fix them. One of the discarded items was a primitive automatic dishwasher, from the 1920s or 1930s. Duane put pieces together, got a motor from his father, and made the dishwasher spray water. It was like a lawn sprinkler in a box. We tried it for dishes and it worked, sort of. It was definitely not a model or brand that ever made it big. Later we used that dishwasher to hold chicken feed.

But patriotism and money called. World War II was on and the call went out for scrap iron, to melt down and build ships and tanks and defeat the Huns and the Japs. That was a no-brainer. Win the war, get rid of the junk, and make money all at the same time. So my father would put the trailer out and my friends and I would load it up. One time I remember we got $1.92, which was big money for little kids. Between the full basement with its dark corners, and the barn's two floors, and the back rooms and the chicken coops and dark places under the stairs and even the overhead crawl spaces, we filled up several trailer loads.

We had to fight rats in the back room. All old houses and farmsteads in those days had rats, I am sure. We poisoned and trapped and sealed up holes. Once a rat seeking chicken feed got caught in the inner workings of the dishwasher and I squished him. The most adventure was when we would get a rat trapped in that back room. Father would seal off whatever hole the rat got in through, and then he and I would go after it with shovels or hoes or whatever. Meanwhile my mother would hide out in the farthest part of the house. We also did that with possums in the chicken coop but they were easier to get because they would play dead.

In grade school we played a lot of pretend games. We fought World War II; we fought the frontier Indian battles; we fought gangsters in the city. We also "explored." After we had explored pretty much everything there was to explore at 711 Hawpatch we branched out. We explored abandoned houses, woods, Walter's swamp, various fields. I can't remember that we ever paid much attention to property lines. We considered all of LaGrange common property, more or less.

This was in the days before television and before we worried much about school work. All the time after school and on Saturdays was available to do whatever we wanted. We played ball a lot. I often played ball by myself. What we called our back porch was a cement slab with a blank wall on one end. I was an infielder. I threw the tennis ball against the wall to create ground balls and line drives. I would back hand the ground smash and make a dramatic throw to first. Of course I was the batter, the shortstop, the pitcher and the first baseman. I could play whole games that way.

I could do ground balls against the barn also but that was dirt and grass and gravel. The barn was better for fly balls and pop flies. I would throw the ball high to come down on the roof to create the pop flies. Not infrequently the ball went over the roof into no-man's land behind. That's where we kept trash before Father hauled it off in the trailer (no city trash pick-up for us). Weeds were back there also. That meant the ball was sometimes lost. Those were the times I bargained with God: "God, help me find this ball and I will be extra nice to my sisters tonight." If I were desperate (usually when it was the only ball) I would promise to volunteer to do dishes. I never told my mother my helpfulness was not necessarily out of love but to keep a deal with God.

When I was twelve my Father bought me a bike. It was a used bike. He paid $10 for it. He told me he did not get his first bike until he was 18. My daughter Cris got a bike at age five and my grandson Jacob got a bike at age three. No delayed gratification any more for modern kids. Most of my friends, and most of the kids in town, whether friends or not, had bikes by the time I got mine.

Before the bikes, Duane, Raymond, and I were pretty much confined to wherever we could walk. With the bicycles we had the whole town to explore, as well as the surrounding area as far as the bike could go (and get back again). Sometimes we played bike tag, which I never went for too much because my bike was slow.

During the years on Hawpatch there were a number of neighborhood "clubs." We created these clubs, and made covenants of sorts. One time I remember we cut our fingers so it was a blood covenant. I don't think the idea for that came from the Bible. With the clubs came clubhouses. The easiest clubhouses were holes in the ground lined with boards with a table top or something similar for the roof. When I was in the eighth grade Duane, Raymond, and I had the granddaddy of all clubhouses. It was a hut mansion, complete with grounds. This was not on the Case property but on the Billman property. Billmans across the street had their own five acres which included a ravine. Duane had the gift of carpentering. Raymond was good support. I remember one of my jobs was to dig the latrine. We spend several months on this project. We had a small hut with a stove. We had a look-out tower. The greatest accomplishment was a bridge across the ravine. We had metal boxes hid in the ground for treasure (mostly to store tools).

When fall came we began to worry. Halloween was coming. Kids in town did mischief on Halloween. We speculated whether Healey and his gang would come to destroy our hut and bridge and look-out tower. The more we discussed it the more we convinced ourselves our hut was in trouble. So we devised a plan. We would outwit the enemy. We would disassemble the whole complex in sections and hide the sections in the grass. Healey's gang would then have nothing to destroy. Later we would put it back together again.

We spent considerable time disassembling our hut and our bridge and our lookout tower. Halloween came and passed. As far as we know Healey did not come, nor his gang, nor anybody else to do mischief. By this time it was November; we were busy with other activities and didn't get the hut re-assembled. Then it was winter. By spring it seemed too big a task and so it was never done. That was the end of huts.

The hut experience became, years later, a great sermon illustration both for me and for Raymond (who also went into the ministry). We were our own enemy, undone by fear of something that never materialized.

In the winter when it had snowed the south side of LaGrange

gathered at the hill. I suppose if I saw it today I would not say it was big, but it was big then. And in the days before TV all the kids would sled. One of the first things you would ask Santa for Christmas was for a sled. North LaGrange had Lightning Hill. South LaGrange had Case Hill. And so they came: big kids and little kids and boys and girls, or see who could go the farthest or who could go the fastest and which sled was the best.

When my sisters and I were all grown up, that is, out of high school, my father must have figured we didn't need the hill any more so he proposed to level it off and sell six lots for houses. That brought Mr. Pierce over. Mr. Pierce was never really a part of my parents' circle of friends. He was principal of the high school and our next door neighbor. The Pierces, in fact, were the only other family that shared our block.

I never saw my father reamed out but Mr. Pierce did it.

"How could you do this? What about the kids of this community? This was their only playground...just because your kids are grown."

My father was not easily intimidated. There was still plenty of space to play. And TV was on the way. Kids by that time did not need to form clubs and play pretend games and get cold in the winter with their sleds. They could be entertained indoors. So we—or rather Father—took out the hill and sold six lots and cut out an acre and a half or so from our five acres.

There were only 22 of us that graduated in my senior class at LaGrange High School. There were more of us earlier but they dropped by the wayside. Some had come and gone but eleven of us had been there all twelve years (no kindergarten in those days). We spent all twelve years in one building. We took trips to New York and Washington and Chicago. It was a small enough class that we knew each other's families. When we got together for reunions, especially while my parents were living, my classmates would always ask about my father or my mother.

My parents had what I call the gift of hospitality. I believe it is one of the gifts of the Spirit. A lot of people were in our home for a lot of different reasons. My mother's relatives came a lot, as did my father's relatives. Then there was the Shipshewana gang, and a bridge club that was made up mostly of teachers and Methodists. My friends came; my sisters' friends came. Later my college friends came. I lined them up a couple of years to rake the leaves over Thanksgiving break, eight of them (otherwise I would have had to do it myself). My college roommate, Loren, stayed with me one whole summer. Shirley Studebaker, missionary kid, stayed with us for part of a year.

My mother did music and so my quartet, and my sisters' friends in trios or duets or sometimes kids that wanted to sing a solo, came to our house to be guided by Mother. After a while one of our rooms was called the piano room. My father originally had his study in there until we thought it best for all if he moved out to a space we created in the back room.

I have a sermon or two on hospitality and I use my parents as illustrations. The best sermon is based on Lydia in the Bible. (Acts 1615; "'Come to my house and stay.' And she prevailed upon us"). A number of people who came through our doors expressed thanks later in life for my parents and their home. Some link it to their growth in Christian faith.

After my sisters and I were married the hospitality extended to our families. We went "home" a lot. The children would stay for days, or even weeks. My parents were always available to baby-sit. The swing in the big spruce tree worked for another generation. Our families were together on holidays. We usually played cards, though with Rook cards, not regular playing cards. Our daughter Cris complained she could not find a playing card in the whole house. Things had changed since my parents were regulars in the bridge clubs.

Sometime after I left home I read Paul Tournier's book, *A Place for You*. Tournier, the Christian Swiss psychiatrist, writes of the importance of "place," that is, an actual location where we belong and which gives us stability and grounding. To have no place, as with refugees, or to be ashamed of our place, is to invite spiritual and emotional alienation. So God sends Abraham to a place in order to establish a nation. It was then I understood the importance of 711 Hawpatch. It was always home, going there was always spiritually and emotionally encouraging.

Things changed some after my sisters and I left home, though perhaps not too much.

My father got rid of the chickens. He no longer kept cows or sheep; the garden was smaller, and eventually there was no garden at all. The town council passed an ordinance, which all towns have now, that you could not raise livestock within the city limits. I'm not sure who else was doing it in LaGrange except us, but we had given it mostly up. The ordinance had a grandfather clause. Anyone presently keeping horses or cows or chickens still could, but if you gave it up for six months you gave up the privilege. For a few years Father rented out part of the barn and part of the field for horses. Finally, when he no longer wanted to keep up with the fences, six months passed and he was no longer allowed to keep livestock.

As soon as I left home my father bought a riding lawn mower. He didn't work nearly as hard as I did. My parents also finally bought a TV; I think they got it because of my sisters. I was in college and I railed against the evils of television. No need to worry. They hardly ever watched it, except on Friday nights when Father watched Louis Ruckheiser and the Wall Street report so he could keep up on his stocks.

Sometime in the 1970s Father bought a farm car (from me) with air conditioning. He could have afforded a truck or something nicer but he was never one to spend money. He considered the air conditioning unnecessary. It would be hot; I would ride with him, and ask: "Why don't you use the air conditioning?"

"I don't know," he would say. I don't know either. I think it was a matter of principle: not a good way to spend money. Later, because of Mother, he put central air in the house.

Mother died in 1982 and Father on December 31, 1988. So, like every family, my sisters, Ann and Mary Sue, and I had the task of dividing the property. I was in my final year as a district superintendent. I was very busy but I did have weekends free. So that's when we gathered and divided the accumulation. So just as I did 50 years before, I went into the barn and the back rooms and the basement and cleaned out all the accumulation. The places where we had chickens had only 35 years of accumulation. Neither of my parents threw anything out. I told someone that when I went through my father's sock drawer I found that he must have had 60 single socks. But since I may have had 30 single socks of my own, in Case style, I combined our single socks and came up with several working pairs.

By summer 1990 we were ready for the sale. The auctioneer was Jerry Grog, a classmate of Mary Sue. He was enthused about the prospects for the sale. What he did not know was,

1) my parents were frugal and we didn't have a lot of expensive stuff; thus there were not nearly as many antiques as people thought there would be.

2) most of what was good had been taken by me, my sisters, or the grandkids.

Nevertheless it was a full day's sale. Plenty of parking, plenty of space to spread out tables, a nice big shaded front yard with trees now 120 years old to offer shade for the tables.

We contacted my sister Ann's classmate, Tom Shrock, to sell the house. It was an old house, congloberated, and it had had no serious decorating for 20 years. To tell the truth it was really in bad shape. The barn was in a state of disrepair. Tom shook his head, we might do better to sell off lots, and then sell the house by itself. But that house was still a landmark. "No," Tom said, "let's go for it. List the whole thing. If it doesn't sell, we'll break it into lots."

What price shall we ask? He said, "Well, we have never had a house inside the city limits of LaGrange to sell for $100,000. Let's list it at that, but be prepared to come down."

A lot of people were interested. I don't how many people looked at it. But an unusual couple came along, name of Allen. Mr. Allen was new to town; he came from the city where $100,000 was not that much for a house. Mr. Allen ran a factory in Shipshewana. They were looking for a place with a lot of room in a prominent location where they could show off their antiques, collections and hobbies. What he wanted to do was display his railroad stuff, including a real for sure railroad crossing with lights flashing, a signal and a drawbar. This was it. They offered the full $100,000. They then spent a lot more improving the property than they paid for it. They tore down the barn and replaced it with a bigger barn.

Most people rejoice when they list a house and it sells immediately and they get full price. But I confess I felt sadness. I thought we would have it a little while longer. Well, we came back and cleaned up the place and finally the day came when we had to leave for the last time. It was fall 1989. We had had that house nearly 50 years. I put the key in the lock and it hurt so much I could hardly turn the key. It was the hardest thing I ever did. It is tough to lose a Mother, and tough to lose a Father, but this was like Father and Mother and home. The word is grief. Mental anguish and suffering caused by pain.

I reread Tournier's *A Place for You*. Despite the importance of place, God never wants us to stay. We establish and recognize our place only so we can then leave it. Because there are new places where God wants us to be.

I still dream about 711 Hawpatch, much less now of course than previously. I have some what I call derivative dreams, where I moving to an old house and am trying to sort through all of the old things left there. And sometimes I am planting a garden.

Riley Leander Case 1896-1988

Riley L. Case - 1980

"I can't believe he just did that." These were my words, spoken to myself, and not to anyone else. These are not thoughts a person shares, at least immediately, lest they be deemed inappropriate.

My father had just died. Well, perhaps not "just died"; he died a short time before. I did my appropriate initial amount of grieving before admitting I was awestruck.

It was not that he died that was so impressive. It was how and when and under what circumstances he died. It was like he had written the script as to how it would happen. It was like he called the shot, like Babe Ruth when he pointed to the stands in 1932 and then hit the home run.

My father was 86 years old when Mother died. It was a surprise really, that she should die first. He who calculated everything in advance had missed on the order of death. Men die younger, Father reasoned. He was four years older than Mother. He brought it up from time to time, even in my presence, as to what Mother should do when he died. Mother was horrified. She lived in denial, as if death would never happen. She didn't want to talk about it. So Father shrugged his shoulders and carried on.

Then she died first. What would happen to him?

No problem. He would carry on. He got along famously (as will be reported later in the chapter). But it could not last forever.

We worried. I worried. He was in our big house at 711 Hawpatch, 82 miles from the nearest family member. A good neighbor said he would look out after him. This worked for a couple of years; then the neighbor died. Another friend said he would check on Father. That worked for a couple of years until that friend died. So no one was looking out for Father.

He slowed after age 92. The doctor had wanted him to exercise and so he did, a walk once around the block at 711 Hawpatch. He admitted one day that it was hard work. He could hardly make it around. That was not good news.

He still drove everywhere. To my sister Mary Sue's in Eldridge, Iowa. To my sister Ann's in Seymour, Indiana, and to our home in Marion, Indiana. Then one day he admitted that he had gotten confused in making the trip to Marion and had wondered off route somewhere. That sent alarm bells ringing. We determined that he should not make the trip any more alone. He agreed, which bothered even more. If he was concerned then we were concerned. And if he could not drive to Marion it would not be long before he would not be able to drive anywhere.

So a week before Christmas in 1988 our son Jeremy drove to LaGrange to bring Father to Marion. The plan was he would stay through Christmas. The family Christmas gathering with my sisters and their families would be in Marion on New Year's Eve, Saturday, December 31. Then Father complained of not feeling well. It was the flu or something. After Christmas he went to the hospital. He was getting not better but weaker. He visited well, but admitted he felt "punk" (his favorite word for "awful"). On Friday our son-in-law Jeff, the doctor looking after Father, reported that Father's systems were shutting down, and asked if I knew what that meant. I said "yes." But Father was still alert. I did not think death would come soon.

My sisters and their families were all coming to Marion on Saturday. They arrived late in the morning and went immediately to the hospital to visit Father. It was not a lengthy conversation. They would be back. Nonetheless, he had seen them. Three minutes later, before they were even in the parking lot, he died. They called me from the hospital even before my sisters and their husbands made it to our house. I admit only now, years later, I had a sense of relief. I dreaded the thought of a long, painful death, like Mother's.

Then I thought, "What has just happened? I can't believe he just did that."

He planned it very well. Or did he? We don't die on cue, do we? God determines the time and the place. Of course, but, knowing my father, he would not be above thinking through just how God might do it. He died with the whole family home. He died without a lot of pain. He died before he would soon be unable to drive and before he would have to leave his home.

We shared the news with our children, on that New Year's Eve; then we had our family dinner. Those present, twenty of us at that time (twenty years later the number would be over 90), opened presents, made plans for the funeral and what needed to happen in the days ahead. After the evening meal, people left for home. Early Sunday I drove to LaGrange. I was scheduled to preach in my home church on New Year's Day, Sunday, January 1, 1989. I was the one who announced my own father's death to the congregation.

I was serving as a district superintendent at the time. I was busy, but at least had some week-ends free. And so on week-ends during the next months my sisters and I started going through the house.

There were some surprises. I believe there were not too many surprises when Mother died. She was more transparent than Father and what was reflected in the personal belongings we went through, including what was expressed by the people who spoke and wrote about her at her death, was fairly consistent with the person we knew.

This was not entirely the case with my father. For all my years with him I did not realize the extent to which he was methodical and purposeful. Young sons don't analyze their father's personalities. I knew he spent hours sitting at his desk, surrounded by files and bookcases. But I never thought much about what he did there.

What he did there was to keep records, voluminous records. About every conceivable subject. And so, after his death, we found amazing records. There were notebooks outlining when he shaved, and how long it was since the last shave. There were notebooks outlining how much time was spent in exercising each day, what the exercises were, and how he felt afterwards. There were notebooks on the service calls on all household appliances. There were notebooks on Rotary activities, on Historical Society activities, on Sunday school class activities, and on sermons heard and articles read.

There were thirteen file drawers full of files. There were files on every conceivable farm-related subject, from timber to crop rotation to land values. There were extensive files on the research done on various stocks. There were obviously files on all the organizations he was connected with: Historical Society, Mental Health, Council on Aging, Rotary, the local church, the annual conference, Purdue ag alumni, The Republican party, the Woodruff cemetery, the Woodruff school reunion, the Corn School reunion.

Account books recorded the spending of every single penny (earlier ones record 1 cent items) from the 1910's on. We know how much he smoked because of the line item recorded simply as "habit." We know when he quit smoking because "habit" no longer appeared in the account books. We know how often he went to Sunday school in the early years (about every other week) because of the entry "S.S. 1 cent." (He was never overly generous.)

He not only kept record of how much Mother spent on phone calls to her sisters, but on which sister got most of the calls (her twin sister Selma).

All of this was carefully organized in a logical system, which was sometimes too complicated to follow. We could not find the title to the car and looked in every conceivable place, from the lock box to the file on autos and "Important Papers." We finally found it in the file marked "Insurance" mixed in with outdated policies. There was a note (there were many notes) indicating that since he had filed the last title away where he couldn't find it, it would put this one in the most logical place. I later found his previous car title filed under "Investments."

The Riley L. Case story can best be told by five periods in his life. 1) Case history; 2) Life before Mother; 3) Active years until retirement; 4) Retirement to Mother's death; 5) After Mother's death.

1. CASES, LAGRANGE COUNTY, AND THE FARM

If my mother can only be understood by understanding Berne, the Mennonites and Fundamentalism, my father can only be understood by understanding Case history, LaGrange County, and the farm.

The Cases first arrived in the new world from England in 1636, not quite on the Mayflower, but close to it. They had been Puritans in England. One relative, Thomas Case, spent time in the Tower of London for theological irregularities. The Cases in the New World intermarried with Spencers and Viets and Holcombs and Humphreys and other New England colonial families and acquired and squandered fortunes through seven generations, almost all in the Simsbury, Connecticut region.

Finally, one Charles (who had served as a bodyguard to George Washington) having fallen on hard times, left Simsbury in 1798 and with his son, Zopher (I) came to Warren, Ohio. Zopher married Annie Randol, evidently a woman with some courage because when Zopher died in 1830, Annie Randol Case gathered up three sons, ages teens to early 20s, and with her brother and several of his sons, in 1835 came to LaGrange County. They were among the first settlers. The three Case boys homesteaded on three corners of a country road which was always referred to by my father as "Case Corners." Since I never hard anyone else ever refer to it as that I asked Father one day when was it called Case Corners. He said in the 40s. I thought for a moment and then realized he meant in the 1840s. Today it is better known as 600 E and 400 S.

The Case Corners reference serves as an insight into the way Father (and his sister, my Aunt Gay) thought, especially about things long ago. They had a sweeping view of history. Stories they told, and they knew lots of them, could have taken place in 1960 or 1910 or 1850. Whatever was told them they remembered. A woman I knew discovered one day that she and I were related. Her great-great grandfather was Abraham Eshleman. Thanks to remembering stories my father related, I told her that Abraham, who would have been a great-great-uncle of mine, lived around Adams Lake, and if she wanted more information I would ask my Aunt Gay. I called Aunt Gay (age 98 at the time), who said she would tell me sometime but not on the phone. When I asked her why, she said it wasn't very nice and someone might be listening. What she had to tell happened in the 1860s, long before she or I or anyone else alive at the time was born, and I told her no one cared anymore even if they overheard.

When I preached a revival in 1985 at the Woodruff Grove Church (Father's home church) I took Father one afternoon and we visited Ken Greenwood, the pastor. I asked Ken if he could come up with the old church books. He produced them and Father went over the membership roll of the 1890s and knew about almost everyone on the list, including several he was astonished about because, as he said, he did not remember them as church-types.

Had Annie Randol Case and her sons been smarter, they would have picked better land in LaGrange County. Instead they picked a portion of southeastern LaGrange County where glaciers millennia ago carved out lakes and deposited stones. Especially the stones. There were so many stones that one great uncle, Frank Eshleman, gathered the bigger ones, used them for building fancy homes, and made money.

When the Amish came a few years later they grubbed out the hawthorns and drained the swamps in western LaGrange County and farmed muck, which was much more productive than what the Cases settled on.

It seemed not to matter. Zopher (II) (only 20 years old when he homesteaded), married, had 7 children, in 1856 built a beautiful New England style farmstead patterned after the Connecticut farm home. That home, about which several essays have been written and many stories told, was the center of Case activities until it finally burned nearly 100 years later, in 1947. When it was built Zopher was only 39 but was already a successful farmer. Living in his home in 1856 were 5 living children, 2 or 3 household helpers and any number of hired men. It was already an operation not unlike some southern plantation.

About the same time, Annie Randol put herself and her boys on Case Corners, in 1835, Col. William Cochran came to Milford Township in LaGrange County as another of the first settlers; Cochran was called colonel because he served in the war of 1812. The colonel built a dam and then a water-powered saw-mill on the south end of Long Lake. He also ran a tavern at a place later known as Cochran's Corners which was also a stagecoach stop. The oldest of his ten children was named Margaret. One of his sons became a Spiritualist.

Also, about that same time Francis Asbury Newnam, born 1813, came from Maryland, age 23 or so. He was Methodist, obviously named after, and (his parents) perhaps converted by, Francis Asbury. Caught up in the Methodist revival they freed their slaves and came to LaGrange County. Francis Asbury Newman married Margaret Cochran. They belonged to the East Springfield church.

Meanwhile Joseph Eshleman, German background, Evangelical Association (now United Methodist) came to LaGrange County from Lancaster County, PA, by way of Starke County, Ohio. He arrived in 1849 with his wife Mary (Erferd) and 10 children in a covered wagon. The Eshlemans established the Woodruff Evangelical Church, originally known as Eshleman's Corners.

The Cases, meanwhile, were accumulating land and money. That is, Zopher, the patriarch, did. When his first wife, Amanda, died, in 1863, he married Ann Smith. He was 51; she was 23. She was younger than six of seven children for whom she was the new stepmother. She had had a rough life; she was poor. There was some gossip about a 51 year old man marrying a 23 year old poor girl. From the photos she does not appear to be a trophy wife. He probably married her not for her beauty but because she had energy, could work, could cook, and could handle stepchildren older than she was. She, according to Aunt Gay, referred to her husband not as "Honey Bunch," or "Sweetie Pie," or even "Zoph," but as "Mr. Case."

By 1870, according to the census, Zopher Case, was the second wealthiest man in Johnson township. The census reported that 12 persons lived in the Connecticut farmhouse, including a couple of hired hands, some relatives needing a place to live, and some hangers-on. Zopher's first family, 7 children by Amanda, had left home by that time. He and Ann Smith Case were in the process of adding four more, including my grandfather, Riley C., born 1868.

By 1880 Zopher had accumulated 1,000 acres of land, and was probably qualified to be in today's terms, an agribusiness operation. One wonders today how many men it took to run such an operation.

Later Riley C would describe his father Zopher in this way:

In letters he had not much schooling. But had a world of experience in the business world....He ruled absolute. So when the boys grew up to be men, they generally went for themselves....Dad was an everlasting worker even to the end. He could do any kind of work, make any piece of wagon, shoe the horses, hugh out anything with ax, like barn timber. Brother Leroy said they had hauled the timber out to fence in quarter section in Milford township, that he and a man by name of Hodge split rails together, that Dad could split as many rails as both of them. They counted off ten cuts each. Dad sang songs all day and led them splitting rails. He always knew where to strike. He had a jovial disposition always liked to play cards and dance. Liked to see a good horse race, wrestle or any clean sport. Had a knowledge of men. And generally sensed the action of his boys and other men.

The reference to ruling absolute and the boys going for themselves when grown may be an insight as to why Riley C., in 1888, decided to strike out on his own. His goal: homesteading in Oregon. Later, in 1911, he commented on the day he left LaGrange County:

It was 23 years ago last Feb. It was a pleasant winter day. An aged Father drove a boy down to the R.R. station. The boy was going away to stake a new life—he knew not where and thought less. Life wanted some change from the routine of a big farm where all is hurry, worry, and the work is never done....

But let us see that Father and boy. The Father counted out $100 for the boy who was going 2,000 miles away. Quite a start, but many a boy has started with less.

As the train rolled in the Father and son shook hands. The conductor said, All aboard, and for the first time in his life that boy saw the big tears roll down his Father's cheeks.

The boy went in the car and for the first time thought, Where am I going? I never thought Father cared for me. He never asked me or advised me that it would be better for me to stay at home.

Today I could read the burden of that Father as he drove home to the care of a busy life handling hired help and more than 1000 A of land....

But life in Oregon for Riley C, it seemed, was not to be. In 1893 Zopher died. There must have been some turmoil in settling the estate. It is probably best we don't know all the details. The question was, who would live in the home place? Ann Smith Case, the young widow, surely did not want to run the farm. The boys from the first marriage were well established. Anyway, it would not work for any of them to move in with, or even near, the second wife (later, as indicative of her headstrong ways, she had the body of the first wife dug up and moved in the cemetery so she would be buried next to Zopher). Whatever the intrigue (and it is presumed there was some) the oldest son of the second family, Riley C, was called to give up the Oregon homestead and come home to live in the house and take over the farm; that is, what had not already been deeded to the other boys.

Riley C. then became the patriarch, a task which he seemed quite suited for. He was only 30 when he moved back; but he soon established himself as a farmer as capable as his father, as a family coordinator who maintained friendships with all the half-brothers and sisters, promoted the family reunions, cared for his mother (except when she was caring for him), and kept the dynasty alive.

There, in the Connecticut farmstead, Father was raised and became attached to the land. He was surrounded by relatives: the Cases, the Eshlemans, the Cochrans, the Newmans. The family reunions were an important part of each summer. The 1912 photo of the Eshleman reunion (Father would have been 16 at the time), pictures 90 persons. In about 1980 or so, Father identified them all. Father's comment about the Eshlemans was that they were all neat and orderly, were church goers (8 families lived within buggy distance of the Woodruff Evangelical Church), and they did well in farming. For years he maintained a round-robin letter relationship with a number of the first cousins.

The Cases, on the other hand, if not slovenly, were at least more nonchalant in life-style. They were not church-goers (a matter of sadness). They were also all Democrats, identified in one place as Jeffersonian Democrats. Leroy became the first Democrat ever to be elected mayor at Kendallville in the 1920s.

In 1937 Riley C. decided to retire. He had managed to make it through the Depression, but was greatly affected first of all when Mary (his wife and my grandmother) died in 1935, and then when the big white barn burned, along with some livestock in 1937. When the word came to him that the barn was burning while he was at an auction in Kendallville, his first question (according to my Aunt Gay) was whether the "boy" (meaning me) was all right.

Before the farm sale my grandfather, Riley C, in December, 1937, put his feelings on paper,

IRON WHEELS

If you farm over a period of fifty years it is a sad feeling to have a sale. My father farmed this place for 50 years before me. The buildings were all built low, so they could pitch off the hay and wheat. For 100 years the farm has the wheat drawed in the barn while in the straw. Today the hay and wheat are all handled with rope and slings. So the barns had to have new raised roofs. It is 35 feet from the floor to the hay track in both the big barns.

In clearing up around the place—there are many things that have a history. The vice of old blacksmith shop was hauled away to the old iron

pile. The Father and all the boys used it. We always had a shop and tools that could make most any kind of repair. Dad always kept one or two yoke of oxen on the farm. A yoke and oxen chains are still here, like many other pieces of by gone days. The farm was always a live stock farm. Where a many good colt grew and cattle and sheep were fed and went to market.

We have lived over this age of iron wheels. Born to two Mothers were 14 of us. All have gone now but Clint and me. We have shaken hands with the world of business: we are done with it. And should discharge ourselves of it. The drama has shut in upon us at fourth act. We have nothing here to expect, but in a short time a sick-bed and a dismissal. The end of iron wheels and its generations are gone. It is a new day. The world is moving fast on rubber tires.

2. LIFE BEFORE MOTHER

Families were obviously getting smaller by the early 1900s. At least, for whatever reason, there were only two children in the Riley C. and Mary Eshleman Case home, my father and his sister (my aunt) Gay. The household consisted of numbers more. Following the tradition set by Zopher and Ann, Riley C. and Mary always had hired hands, indoor help, relatives and strays staying with them. Father's cousin, Bernard, for one, stayed and went to school while his parents were homesteading in Canada.

Both Father and Aunt Gay spoke with fondness about growing up years. Father mostly about pets and animals and work and going to school. Aunt Gay, the writer, would pen poems about her home and write about her favorite trees: the young walnut tree halfway down the lane, and the favorite Pound Sweet Apple tree in orchard beyond the chicken coop. She would talk about the scarlet tanagers along the road to school and her classmates in the city (Wolcottvile, pop. 350) who marveled at the farm when they visited.

In 1914 Father entered Purdue University. When the First World War came he worried about whether he should, or would have to, fight. While at Purdue he applied for officers' training school and did not pass the test. He then graduated and took a farm exemption. This bothered him. As late as October, 1923, he wrote,

I let the war business worry me too much. I cannot throw it off as I should, I must do so. I do not blame Hogg, why should I blame myself?

Later, when he applied for the county superintendent of schools and did not get it, he was convinced it was because of criticism that he had not gone into the army.

After two years on the farm Father followed a friend to Grafton, North Dakota where he taught for two years (and bought some land). He then came back to LaGrange County to teach at Shipshewana. He became the first ag teacher in LaGrange County. There appears to have been some intrigue as to how he got the job at Shipshewana, how he soon became the principal at the school, how he was relieved from being principal (that's when he went back to school), and then later, how he got the job back again. Despite all the intrigue he believed (at least at this time in his life) he was shy and introspective. He once commented that Gay met more people and knew more people at Purdue after one month than he did after four years.

Some revealing diary excerpts:

Jan. 8, 1925. *"Read poetry tonight. I am not sure that is a way to improve. It may be good but it don't seem to help me. I like history and sociological problems."*

"I have decided on a course of action. I am either going to be County Superintendent of this county next year or a farmer in Johnson township."

"Still running loose as far as the women are concerned. I am a 'heck' of a fellow. I never have a girl. I wish I could let myself be stricken by some woman like Edna.....When I a fellow gets as old as I, he can't run with all the women. He soon gets a reputation and I guess I have mine.....Life is a funny battle after all. I see I am losing my pep. It seems harder to vent my best effort all the time....I realize before I go on the farm though, I ought to have a wife but where I am going to get her. Sis is in the same boat as I. She fools around waiting for the right man to turn up and she is getting older all the time.

July 20, 1926. "*In St. Joe on a new job. No woman, but prospects. I like the place so far. Have a good place to stay but a poor place to eat. Should be doing something to awake this town up.*"

Mother was obviously the "prospect" in the reference.

Sept. 2, 1927. "*At home doing nothing. Do not know which way to go. It seems to me it is a mark of weakness that a man cannot make up his mind.*"

The same entry then analyzes (true R.L. Case style) the strengths and weakness of five options that could be a part of his future: 1) medicine; 2) economics; 3) education; 4) farming; 5) business and administration. It would appear at this point that Father was still not sure what he wanted to be when he grew up (he was 31 at the time).

Meanwhile his father, Riley C. was offering advice: in a letter dated November 3, 1927 (Father is at Indiana U.):

…Sorry you think of these 6 years (as wasted*). I would complete that medicine course. It is no harder than 6 years of any kind of work. History builds itself every year. Home here will pass through a good deal. And like others we may take a good deal of care. But will grow more so in the years to come. Life is ever a fight and he with the most nerve will make most for himself. Or leave a path of ruin and destruction… to be paid by the hard earnings of those who save.*

With a profession one is most sure of a good income everyday that will make a good living.…When you put in an education all your time and money life has not been a failure. And I believe…nine farmers out of 10 are not making more than a living.……

Regardless of his father's advice, Riley L. in 1928 changed his mind at the last minute and instead of enrolling in medicine, enrolled in the Master's program in education at Indiana University.

Mother is in the picture at this time and their six-year courtship (if that is what it can be called) is best told by Mother (see the chapter about her). One of Mother's diary entries may tell it all. Mother is

so much wanting Father to confess Christian faith. Father seems
preoccupied about other things.

Edna's diary, Jan. 24, 1926.

*Another miserable day! Go to S.S. Oh those eyes! Have communion and
R. leaves. Hurts me. Don't see why. If I'd have to compose music today I'd
write it in D minor—expressing sadness, agony and distress and misery.*

It is not apparent from the letters and diaries when the
relationship was heating up and when it was faltering. "Then all the
sudden..."

3. RILEY L AND EDNA – 50 YEARS OF MARRIAGE

Mother was determined not to marry a non-Christian and
Father's faith was suspect. He finally made a public confession,
was baptized, and joined the church. Riley L. and Edna were
married December 26, 1931. For their first meal at their home in
Shipshewana Mother fixed soup and Father said he couldn't eat it
because it was too salty. Mother cried. Other than that incident, told
from time to time by Mother (Father never mentioned such things)
the adjustment to marriage must have gone very well.

Riley L and Edna were the unlikeliest of couples, yet their
marriage would have to be considered a roaring success. Mother was
a great affirmer, always with her children, but especially with her
husband. I don't believe I ever heard her openly criticize Father (but
see chapter on Mother). Father began to blossom as an established
member of the community. My parents launched their social life
in Shipshewana. But they also enjoyed her relatives—never mind
Mother did not marry a Mennonite; as the oldest of four sisters but
the last one married, her sisters were just happy to see her married
at all. And they enjoyed Father's relatives, all of whom were skilled
socially.

Father also began his long spiritual journey. He led the
mealtime prayers. He never missed church. He supported Mother
in emphasizing Bible reading for the children. Eventually he taught
Sunday school and served on the church committees.

Other than family, my parent's primary friendship group was the Shipshewana crowd. Fifty years later the Proughs, the Millers, the Reifsniders, the Wolfs, the Hostetlers, the Bakers are still names remembered. They were the landed gentry, if a town of 300 can have a landed gentry. I remember as a child going to Saturday night "parties," which as I remember, were mostly eat and talk. Some of these families were older, some were younger (in fact, had earlier been students of my parents). The group was mostly Methodists, and the problems of the Shipshewana Methodists were, as I recall, often the topic of conversation, although they covered other churches also, as well as the school and the businesses and the scandals. When I read Sinclair Lewis' novel, *Main Street*, I thought to my self, this could be Shipshewana. Even when my parents moved to LaGrange and began to relate to another set of friends, they kept their Shipshewana friends.

It must have been to impress the Shipshewana folks that Mother wore the dead fox. The dead fox was actually a fur pelt wrap, fashionable in the 1930s and 1940s, complete with face, paws, and tail. It was either Mother's idea or Father's (obviously) but my sisters and I cannot figure out which. It simply does not fit with the image of Mother as a sweet Mennonite girl, supposedly not wrapped up in the ways of the world, to wear a dead fox fur wrap. On the other hand, maybe we misread Mother. My cousin Waneta says her mother Selma (Mother's twin sister) remarked on occasions that Edna always was more daring than the rest of the sisters and did things other members of the family would not think of doing. Maybe Mother had a worldly streak. The fox could have been a gift from Father, but Father actually was not given to expensive gifts, especially something as impractical as a dead fox. He normally did not live ostentatiously.

But then again, he did do some impulse buying from time to time (later he bought Mother a mink stole). My sisters (and even I) were cautious about snooping around in Mother's closet because somewhere in there was the dead fox. I knew Mother would not wear it to church, nor in Berne. The only place left was to Shipshewana gatherings where people did not think of Mother as a Mennonite-fundamentalist-dispensationalist-religious person. Later she wore the dead fox to Rotary functions, where it fit well. None of us remember how it got disposed of or when.

My parents survived the Depression in pretty good shape. Father lost money in some banks, but because he never spent money (a trait he passed on), was able to buy two farms and make an investment in the reorganization of the Shipshewana Bank, a decision that upped considerably the value of the estate later on. (Maybe the dead fox was seen as an investment.)

In 1937 the County Agricultural Extension job was offered to Father. I am sure he was not thinking at the time of "God things," but it must have been a "God thing." The job fit like a glove. It offered a match for all of Father's talents, gifts, interests, inclinations, idiosyncrasies and dreams. Extension work was new. LaGrange County had not had a full-time agent before. Father was the ideal person. He would define the office and set the standard.

The extension job allowed him, for example, the opportunity to "run things," which is not identified as one of the gifts of the Spirit in the Bible, but which was an inclination (and a gift) for which he was admirably suited. He could see a problem, envision a plan of action, devise a strategy, recruit the volunteers, make it happen, and keep copious notes as part of evaluation. He promoted and enlarged the 4-H program; he coordinated the 4-H and farm interests at LaGrange's long-time street fair known as Corn School. Since it was held in October it showcased corn and crops. Father later pulled the 4-H program out of Corn School, developed a new fairgrounds site, and started a separate 4-H fair (not without controversy). He organized Rural Youth. He got a Rural Youth Band started. He encouraged Home Economics Clubs; he initiated garden tours and dairy tours and orchard tours and new farming method tours. He organized trips for his 4-Hers and ran the 4-H camp. He started the Rotary Club in LaGrange and then, when he was Rotary governor, sought to start Rotary clubs all across northern Indiana.

In addition to being good at "running things" Father also liked to dispense advice. His first office, in a store front across from the court house, was lined with what appeared to be every pamphlet published by the U.S. Department of Agriculture. Surrounded by all that knowledge he gladly offered himself to all the farmers who came seeking his advice. He was like a guru on the mountain dispensing wisdom on such esoteric topics as corn borers, crop rotation, and pruning raspberries. There was no industry in LaGrange County at that time. The economy was agriculture and Father was the designated expert.

His image of an agricultural guru was enhanced by his regular appearances on the Jay Gould show on WOWO Fort Wayne. Radio was king in those days with only a few stations on the air. WOWO (the clear channel station—which meant you might pick it up in Georgia in the middle of the night) was the dominate station in northern Indiana and surrounding areas. The Jay Gould show was broadcast every weekday at noon. It was a sort of variety show designed for farmers (who supposedly listened when they had come into the house for the noon meal). Nancy Lee and the Hilltoppers and various guests provided music; Jay Gould provided commentary and small talk and hosted the farm experts: county agents, extension people from Purdue, and others. As a child I was greatly impressed; it would be like a television studio today. After a few years the interviews were taped. County agents and other experts came in and expounded on whatever they wanted to expound on, the weather, the price of corn, the record yields, or the elm beetles.

As a ten-year old I was not particularly impressed that my father was important, or that he had touched numbers of lives. That began to change on January 1, 1989, the day after his death. I had been scheduled to preach at my home church in LaGrange. Ruth and I stayed for Sunday school. The Sunday school class Ruth and I visited that day consisted of about 25 persons, mostly in their 50s and 60s. They began to tell stories about my father. All but two (who had moved to LaGrange later) spoke.

They spoke of Riley L. Case of the 1930's and 40's and 50's. They remembered Riley L. Case the disciplinarian principal, who made them stay after school and clean up the gym. They remembered Riley L. Case who kept 4-H kids at the house when the snow storm was too bad to go home; and Riley L. Case who persuaded teenagers to go to 4-H camp and got them interested in Rural Youth. Then they spoke of Riley L. Case of the 1980s, with all of his idiosyncrasies. They did a lot of laughing. At one time Father probably knew more people in LaGrange County than any other person. This included a number of Amish friends.

Riley L and Edna were excellent parents. Father taught work, money management, and discipline. Mother taught Bible, music, and prayer. When I was six years old Father brought home the first chickens. They were only partly for eggs. They were mostly to teach me responsibility and work. I would never have an allowance. I was to earn all my spending money, which consisted of whatever the eggs brought when sold. So at six years old I was putting feed into chicken feeders and gathering eggs. Father paid for the chickens and the feed.

4. RILEY L AND EDNA – RETIRMENT

Father celebrated 25 years of County Extension work in LaGrange County in 1962 and retired in 1964. He retired at age 68. He might have retired earlier but—and I confess some questioning of motives here—there were some other factors at work (or so I suspect). Probably because they had their children later in life, and since many of their friends were younger, people thought my parents were not as old as they really were. Mother delighted in that. When people asked their age, Mother never told them and Father was under strict instructions not to do so either. When Mother's twin sister Selma died, Rev. Yates, pastor at LaGrange, asked Mother how old her sister was. Mother believed it was a trick to get her to tell her age, and she answered, "The same age I am." Even at age 80 Mother would not admit she was eligible for senior citizen status.

Mother, in fact, taught school a couple of years after Father retired. That worked, for Father was prepared to devote full-time to his new job, serving as Rotary Governor. He had planned (as usual) how he would spend retirement and so he did whatever political maneuvering was necessary to get elected district president. He tackled his Rotary job the way he did all jobs: he set goals for the clubs, worked to start new clubs, and traveled around the northern third of Indiana giving his standard speech, which was, how agriculture had changed in the last 50 years.

It was a good speech, given many times. When he was first a county agent, he organized corn shucking contests, and refereed between the farmers favoring horses and the farmers favoring tractors. The map in his office tracked the R.E.M.C. progress in bringing electricity to rural areas. He traced the advance in corn yields from 75 bushels to the acre to 100 to 140 to 170 and chicken operations from 20 hens in every farm family to 10,000 hens on just a few farms.

He also decided to get more involved in church work. In 1971, when he was 75 years of age, he went for the first time in his life to the North Indiana Conference of the United Methodist church as the delegate from LaGrange. Age 75 is when most laypeople phase out. Preachers are has-beens at 65. I remember thinking, "My goodness, it takes even preachers 10 years of attending conference to figure out what is going on." I thought, "He is past his prime; he won't know anyone; I'm going to have to stick close, look out for him, explain what is going on, introduce him to people."

It was just one of many times my father surprised me. I had been attending conference for nearly 25 years, but it soon seemed he knew more people than I did. Instead of my introducing people to him he was introducing people to me. All kinds of people, strangers to me, seemed to know him, many because of his years on WOWO with Jay Gould, others because of Rotary connections, others because of extension work, others because of Purdue ag relationships, others because he had been a former high school teacher and principal and had former students scattered around. And finally and not least by any means, he uncovered first and second cousins of my mother that I never knew existed (she had over 100 first cousins spread around and I have no I idea how many second cousins that gives me).

It so happened that year, 1971, was the year that the conference elected delegates for General and Jurisdictional Conferences. The laity needed to ballot for sixteen lay delegates (with 800 lay delegates present). They always, it seemed, elected prominent lay leaders who had served on conference committees, had attended conference for years, and made speeches. This year was different. My father was a newcomer in conference politics; he was in his mid-70's at a time when a premium was being placed on youth; he was, as far as I knew, unknown. When he started getting votes the bishop assumed people were confused and were voting for Riley Case the clergyperson (the bishop was one who did not know him), and remarked as much (and was corrected by a number of people). Frankly, I assumed so too, though in those years I was not well known myself. This was a misreading of the situation. Father was simply known far and wide and at age 75 he was elected to the Jurisdictional Conference. This started several years of activity in the annual conference.

Father also became more or less (mostly less) involved in politics. The Cases had been Democrats ever since Zopher came to Indiana in 1835, and very possibly long before that. They had been such strong Democrats that they opposed the Civil War ("If Lincoln wants a war let him fight it") and several (at least two) of the older Case boys (half-brothers to Riley C.) fled to Canada rather than to be conscripted.

But this changed in 1940 when the family turned Republican. The "family" is this instance was for sure Riley C., Riley L., and Aunt Gay. It is unknown at least to us now whether there were other uncles and cousins who changed. The reasons are a bit vague (though at the time it is certain they were not vague). Aunt Gay always said it was because her dad (Riley C, still the patriarch) declared that no man, good president or not, deserved a third term (referring to FDR). The Cases always discussed (or argued) politics when they were together. Unfortunately, I was too young to follow the conversations.

So they became Republican, and rather conservative Republicans at that. Father always liked Robert Taft from Ohio. He was ready to launch a political career himself about the time he retired from being county agent, and was lined up to be nominated for some county job--I think county commissioner--but uncharacteristically, forgot the meeting the night the caucus was making the decision and was consequently passed over by the party. He could laugh about it later.

After the stint as Rotary governor Mother and Father had another 15 years of enjoying retirement. They traveled, frequently making trips to Florida and other places with Mother's sisters and husbands, and several times overseas, usually with something connected with Rotary. However, Father never could handle more than a week in

Florida. He had too much to do at home. Too much to do was a reference to managing the farm, following the stock market, keeping accounts, filing information in the file folders, staying active in all his clubs, and being present for the grandchildren.

5. LIFE AFTER MOTHER

Mother's death was quite a blow to Father. For one thing his carefully-laid life plan had not followed its predicted course. He always assumed he would die first. He didn't. She did. So when she died (May 31, 1982) he was at least momentarily at a loss to know what to do. I believe he thought he could not cook and he could not stand living alone. Despite the fact that Father was strong-willed it was apparent that Mother had made a lot of the decisions about what to wear, what to eat, and where to go.

That indecision was short-lived. He could not see himself, nor could the rest of us, in any other place than on Hawpatch Street in LaGrange. He would be lost without his 13 file cabinet drawers of files, and where could he go that he could take them all? So he stayed and took care of the house by himself.

True to his style, he planned how it might work. He was not one to clean (Mother had always done that) so he would have to hire a housecleaner. But he was also not about to spend too much money on a housecleaner. Once a month would be adequate. But what about the beds? Mother had changed sheets once a week. Father's solution was to sleep in each of the four upstairs bed rooms for a week at a time and when the housecleaner came she could change and wash all four beds at once.

Cooking was another problem. When his father, Riley C, became a widower in 1935, (and lived a widower for 12 years) he cooked. He had to. He had hired hands. His too was an open house. People came to visit. When they came he prepared the meals. He would fix Sunday dinner for our family, for example (and cook the potatoes with the skins on). Father would not follow in his father's footsteps. So Father became a regular at the A & W restaurant. It was never a quick lunch. It usually involved visiting with whoever the other patrons were.

Whether deliberately planned or not (probably not) Father made lots of changes and soon had launched himself in what turned out to be a whole new life style. If we thought that Mother's death would a reason for him to slow down, we were mistaken. The opposite, in fact, took place. Freed from restraints laid on by my mother (both good and bad) his idiosyncrasies were free to roam widely over the landscape, and so they did. He went more places, talked to more people, and did more things than he ever did before.

One of the youth counselors told us that when the youth planned an all-night party at church, Father was curious and asked if he could stop by. He did, at 11:30 P.M. and stayed for an hour or so. We— Ann, Mary Sue, and I—used to worry when we called him late at night and there was no answer. We could find out the next day where he had been.

One of the first things he did was to join Senior Citizens and Council on the Aging (even at age 80 Mother would not admit she was a senior citizen). Both groups, if I am reading the situation correctly, he soon dominated. He not only joined the Senior Citizens but soon carried the mens' section in the Senior Citizens choir. Mother, who had the gift of music, would have been horrified. Though she encouraged Father in most of his endeavors she never did encourage him much in public singing.

Mother would also have been horrified to know that he soon began to shop the rummage sales. My sisters, Ann and Mary Sue, and I worried about what he wore and how he acted on such occasions. His favorite pair of shoes he bought at the church rummage sale. The only new clothes he had were bought by his children, some of which he wore and some of which he didn't. He wore his favorite unmatching outfits far beyond when they should have been cleaned.

The year he was 90 I saw his 4-H fair schedule. Work every night from 5:00-9:00 in the Methodist food booth on the French fryer; work at the Purdue ag dinner; work at the Republican Party booth; work at the Historical Society booth. Not on the official schedule was: visit with people throughout the week.

The summer of the year he died (1988), when Father could hardly walk, Ruth and I visited LaGrange and dad wanted to take us to the fair (we weren't too excited but went). He couldn't walk around with us but wanted us to leave him in the pavilion while we walked around. Unknown to us the queen contest was in the pavilion. When we checked back he wanted to stay for more of that so we walked around some more. We came back much later (and felt guilty about how late we were) worried because of the heat (excessive) and the crowd. Father was on the front row taking notes on all the candidates (enjoying the swim suit competition). When I went to get him he asked if we could stay a bit longer for the final act!

Every year he worked the Rotary fish fry and sold twice as many tickets as anyone else. He visited the Amish enough that he was one of the few "English" I know who was invited to attend an Amish wedding (an all-day affair through which he slept much of time).

He also became known for giving farm tours. Of course every drive in the car with him was a farm tour. His non-stop commentary consisted mostly of who lived in the white house we were passing, who lived there before that, and who lived there before that, and whatever happened to them. Houses where Eshlemans or Cases or any relatives once lived inspired commentary about the relatives. When he gave farm tours he would lecture on what makes a "family farm." To illustrate he would visit his Amish friend, Jerry Otto, who raised 13 children on 80 acres. Of course the stop at Jerry Otto's home included ongoing lectures by Jerry himself, who had his own wisdom to dispense.Jerry farmed the old-fashioned way, with all the animals: chickens, cows, horses, sheep, and the gardens and various crops. Then Father would take his tour guests one half mile down the road to Ernest Youngs. Ernest's family farm consisted of over 1,000 acres, a couple of sons, and lots of expensive equipment.

Perhaps our family was most surprised by Father's Christian commitment those last years. We always wondered whether much of his Christian involvement was primarily because of Mother. If so at the beginning it was not so at the end. I remember being surprised one Sunday when Father saw a farmer out in the field on the Sabbath and launched into a lecture on desecrating the Sabbath that would have done justice to any preacher.

I was a district superintendent during this time and had to conduct charge conferences in churches. The charge conference is the yearly business meeting which is boring enough if its your own charge conference, let alone if it is someone else's. Father wanted to go along, and, to my amusement, from time to time offered a public opinion.

He evidently showed up for everything that went on at the church. Since he offered strong opinions about most of what went on I feared that he was becoming obnoxious. Once the preacher did call me with such a concern. I believe it is more accurate, however, to suggest that the church accepted (if they did not always agree) with what he had to say because by his faithfulness and his age he had earned the right to say it.

In addition to what went on at the United Methodist church he attended other churches and services. Mother had started this church-visiting during the years when she wanted more from church, and especially Bible teaching, than what she was getting at the Methodist church. The Sturgis (Michigan) Bible church was her favorite. They would attend not only Sunday nights but for special services.

Father not only maintained this church-visiting, he upped the intensity. He began attending churches Mother would never been seen in. She didn't want anything too emotional. She was not into Wesleyan or Nazarene or Church of God services. Father attended them all. He was in church every Sunday night somewhere. He became the official "pray-er" at a lot of non-church functions. He started attending some services that would have horrified Mother, most specifically, Full Gospel Businessmen's meetings (a charismatic group). The most gratifying comments by far at the funeral home and the funeral (about 300 people signed the register) were those about Riley L. Case the Christian. All kinds of preachers showed up who told us about Father attending their services (places I never suspected). A man said he hardly knew Father but he had heard him pray at Full Gospel prayer. One woman, on the Sunday after he died on Saturday, told me at church that, that very morning, she woke up not intending to attend church then thought to herself, "If I don't show up Riley Case will miss me." A number of others mentioned his habit of talking with everyone, including the children. His files contained written ideas and notes on sermons and books, notes that we never knew existed.

Then there were the widows. He never spoke of these. We only knew about them because when we would be visiting in LaGrange he would get phone calls. When I asked once who it was he gave a vague answer. The next time we saw him he repented for lying and admitted it was one of the women who called him frequently.

And the farm? Well, we still have the farm. In true Riley L. Case style he had it all planned out. He wanted the farm to stay in the family; he did not want it sold or broken up. After all, it had been in the family ever since it was first homesteaded by Zopher Case. But he figured that on our own the family could not make this happen. His solution: incorporate the farm and issue stock to all the children and in-laws and grandchildren. He did this fifteen years before his death. He insisted on following all of the laws of the state of Indiana for corporations. We had a board of directors, which met regularly; we had a stockholders' meeting which met regularly (usually at Christmas when the family gathered). We kept minutes and filed all the necessary reports. Knowing that we would have to work with renters he even devised a formula for what the rent should be. The formula involved average yields of corn and soybeans, and the price of December corn and November beans at the Wolcottville Elevator Company on May 15, all calculated to determine each year's rent.

In November, 2009, my sisters, their husbands, and Ruth and I traveled through Iowa for four days. We have gone on cruises other years. We have traveled to other places some years. One of the incentives for getting together (besides just have fun) is to conduct our farm business. And so we do. We also eat a lot, laugh a lot, and talk about Mother and Father, our heritage of faith, and how that is being passed down to our children and grandchildren; and we talk about growing up in LaGrange County.

The Messiah And Mennonite Evangelism

"He shall feed his flock like a shepherd..."

I was in my truck making an uneventful trip to town. The Christian radio station was on. It was before Christmas.

"...and he shall gather the lambs with his arms..."

It was the alto aria from the *Messiah*. The alto finished. It was the soprano's turn:

"Come unto Him, all ye that labour and are heavy laden, and He shall give you rest...."

I reflected: the same melody, but a different voice. The same melody, but a different key. The same message, but a different covenant. The Old Testament and the New. The promise. The invitation. The gospel. I was overwhelmed with emotion. I slowed the truck, lest my inattention to driving be a hazard to others.

When the soprano was finished I waited for the next number. It would be the choir's turn. They were the exhorters, the cloud of witnesses, the heavenly host: *"His yoke is easy and His burden is light..."*

That was too much to ask, even for Christian radio. The music changed to fa-la-la songs and seeing the little town lie still-we and the stars going by silent-ly.

I felt cheated. Part the First is not complete without the chorus. I turned off the radio and finished it myself. I sang the soprano and the alto and the tenor and the bass, and directed them all, one hand on the wheel, one hand directing, and in my mind I spoke to the choir so they would get it right: "Lightly, lightly, the yoke is easy. This is grace as against law. You don't sing this like the Volga Boat Song."

The seats were hard as I first remember them, in the Big Church, the Mennonite Church in Berne, Indiana. And there were lots of seats, enough for 2,000 people, more if they were children, more if you counted the choir, room for more people in that church than there was population in the town; and the seats were always filled, at least for the *Messiah*, with people on extra chairs. Sometimes the newspapers estimated crowds of 3,000, but that was in the days before fire marshals.

I remember being sleepy. It was hard to sleep when you are a little boy, when it is crowded and hot and the seats are hard. Methodist churches were discovering padded pews. Services seemed not quite so long with padded pews, and little children could sleep. But in the Big Church the seats were hard.

It only stood to reason. There would be no padded pews in the Big Church. In the 1860s, as I later read, the church had nearly split over the issue of tassels on buggies. Mennonites were plain people. Too much luxury meant compromise with the world. Any church which argued over tassels on buggies would never tolerate padded pews. Later in reflecting on it, I wondered whether my people, my great-grandparents and great-great uncles, and the myriads of ancestor cousins, were on the pro-tassel or anti-tassel side.

The *Messiah* was always long. Mennonites, so I came to believe, found no virtue in brevity. Methodists were programmed for one-hour services. God and the preacher could have their hour, but not ten minutes more and preachers, if they did not know this already, after one hour were on their own time. Not so for Mennonites. Mennonites, I am sure--at least for my cousins and the boys I knew--did not care for long services either. But they would never say so. To complain was unseemly, or even sinful. Mennonites did not believe in penance but they practiced it. One needed to suffer on hard seats as the sun passed across the sky to restore the proper relationship with God. The *Messiah* went on and on, as if the message was so great that nothing should be left out. And if it were left out one year, it was so it could return another.

When I was old enough to read I would follow the program, figuring how much more time before we got to the end, which was the "Amen Chorus." But I forgot, at least several years running, that just because we had come to the Amen Chorus, did not mean we were ready to quit. The Amen Chorus took six pages of music, with sopranos and tenors and altos and basses each taking turns, going up and down the scale, a round and then a few more rounds, the sopranos lingering on a high A natural. Six pages of Amen was itself equal to two whole anthems in a Methodist church. But of course it was logical. Amen does not really mean the end. It means so be it. And if we sang about the gospel, so be it, and be it, and be it, and be it, and be it.

I was not brought up to question my parents' decisions, but the frequent pilgrimage--and that is what it was, not a trip, but a religious pilgrimage--from my home in LaGrange, Indiana, to Berne, Indiana, 82 miles south, not 83 or 81 but 82--about the same distance as from Nazareth to Bethlehem--on the first Saturday of December, was not my idea of Christmas celebration, at least in the early years.

My father must have felt the same way. He did not always come with us. He was busy, or something. I suspect now, years later, that he found reasons to be busy. This sort of music was not in his genes. It was in my mother's genes, but not his. He was not blessed by six pages of the Amen Chorus. But he did his duty—usually.

My mother came almost always, even during the war. We needed coupons because of gas rationing. We were told to make only necessary trips. For Mother to experience the *Messiah* was a necessary trip. Sometimes we stayed over. Sometimes we visited with cousins and then came home and arrived at 2:30 in the morning.

There were no children's nurseries in those days of hard pews, at least for the *Messiah*. My sisters would be on one side of my parents--sometimes they got the lap—and I would be on the other. Mennonites didn't believe in nurseries. Methodists invented nurseries, I am convinced. They were places to dump the kids while adults enjoyed, or at least tolerated, church. For Mennonites, hard pews and long services and no nurseries, were the price one paid for being holy. Mennonites talked about suffering, and their kids experienced it.

My relatives sang in the *Messiah*, my Aunt Selma and Uncle Wilbur, and various other great-uncles and great-aunts and first cousins once removed, and second cousins twice removed. My mother had 83 first cousins on her mother's side and second cousins like the sand of the sea; that side of the family alone with spouses and in-laws and children and nieces and nephews must have made up a big part of the 200 or so--one year I counted to pass the time, there were 220--in the choir. I know there were more people in the choir alone than were in my church's whole congregation back in LaGrange.

The church seemed designed for the choir. The new building in 1912 was erected with a big bowl, a sounding board, for a choir of 200, built in a semi-circle. And right in the middle, where in some churches there would be an altar, or at least a cross, there was a grand piano. No crosses in this Mennonite church, just a pulpit and a grand piano.

The Big Church, 1915, with the featured grand piano

Freeman Burkhalter, Mother's cousin (on her father's side), was the director. He had always been the director as far as I knew, and he would continue to be the director, for another 50 years from when I first remembered him. Freeman had left Berne to go to Moody Bible Institute and Northwestern University and eventually to Columbia University to get a doctorate. Then, instead of going to some university to teach, he came back to Berne, to the Big Church, to direct the Men's Chorus and the Women's Chorus and organize various trios and quartets and sextets, to the glory of God. He also taught fourth graders in school the violin and directed the high school choir, which always won in state competition.

Of course they would win in state competition. Mennonite teenagers had music in their genes. They could join the choral society and after "And the Glory of the Lord shall be revealed, and all flesh shall see it together"—after that, and six pages of the "Amen" Chorus, high school music was a snap. The choir traveled one year to Switzerland, back to where their great grandparents had come from, back where there were fourth cousins who spoke a different language and lived in the mountains and worshipped in a different kind of church. The burgermeister served as tour host.

In the mid-eighteen hundreds the ancestors had migrated to Indiana--extended families, whole churches. In 1868 the church cast lots to determine who the new preacher should be. A 17-year old boy was chosen. They called him "Sammie." He was a Sprunger, like many in the town. He took his chosen-ness seriously. He went off to school. He came back wearing a necktie. The congregation was aghast. But he was chosen, was he not? The message was clear: the spirit of Christ, not clothing, was the essence of the faith.

In 1886, revival broke out and continued for three months. Several hundred were converted. The young people, so it is reported, walked the streets singing. They formed a choral society. They sang the German oratorios, *New Jerusalem* and *Creation*, the *Messiah*, and *Elijah*. Eventually the *Messiah* would prove to be the most popular and it was repeated every year.

The choral society must have sung originally without an organ. But the organ finally came. Some old-timers wept, but the young people were singing. A German Temperance Society (oxymoron?) was formed. In the early 1900s the saloons closed, not without conflict. The Swiss-Germans gave up their beer and the town went, for all practical purposes, dry.

In 1905 the Big Church asked the other churches of the community to join it in Union Meetings. Charles Gabriel was song leader the first year (the same year he wrote "I Stand Amazed in the Presence"). In the years to come the best known evangelists, men like Wilbur Chapman, Billy Sunday, Paul Rader, and R. A. Torry, would speak, and the best known song evangelists, like Homer Rodeheaver would accompany them. The town would take on the flavor and the theology of the fundamentalist preachers who ministered there. While the outside world was reporting that the fundamentalist-modernist controversy was over, and the fundamentalists had lost, the crowds were overflowing the big building.

Sammie finally retired for good in 1914, forty-six years after he had first been chosen by lot. The church was to be known as the largest Mennonite Church in the world, its Sunday school the second largest Sunday school in Indiana. Even in the 1950s the Sunday school would average 1,300. The five-weeks community Bible school would enroll as many as 700 children. Bolstered by imports such as my sisters and me, the enrollment in Bible school would exceed the enrollment in public school. And always, on the first Saturday in December, the *Messiah* would be sung.

When Freeman came back from the university, barely 30 years old, they gave him the *Messiah* to direct. Sometime in the 1950s, because the crowds were so big, a Sunday afternoon performance was added. That's how in the course of 60 years Freeman directed the Messiah 100 times. I was there the weekend he did the 100th in the 1990s, an old man working without a music stand or a text. He stood by the piano. There was no podium. No signals to the choir to get their attention. No nodding to the organist. No distractions. No applause. No bowing. No attention to director or soloists or organist. The music itself was everything.

I don't remember when, in the process of experiencing all of this, that the transformation began to take place, that the *Messiah* became something more than a long evening with boring music. I think it started with the "Hallelujah Chorus." I learned early in the scheme of things that at one point in the long evening everyone stood. They did not rise slowly, looking around to check to see if this was indeed the right moment, as if fearing that they might stand and be the only ones. The first chord and they rose as one person.

Even a young boy was impressed. I asked my mother why people stood. She said, "Because of Jesus." She didn't mention great music. She didn't speak of the story of a king long ago who stood up. People stood for Jesus. When you sing about Jesus the Messiah reigning forever and ever with the angels and the saints and the martyrs, as in the book of Revelation, you stand. It made sense.

One day someone asked my Uncle Wilbur why the *Messiah* had made such an impact. "Because," Uncle Wilbur answered, "it's all Scripture. It's the gospel."

I doubt if that was the kind of explanation printed in the program when the *Messiah* is sung at Radio City Music Hall. But the Berne Mennonite Church was not Radio City Music Hall. For Uncle Wilbur and others if the *Messiah* was great it was because it was the gospel. It was the story of salvation. Uncle Wilbur commented one day the *Messiah* should be done on three nights, not just one. Part I for Christmas. Part II for Good Friday. Part III for Easter. Incarnation, Atonement, Resurrection.

The Atonement was the crucial part. *"Behold the lamb of God... that taketh away the sins of the world..."* *"He was despised and rejected. A man of sorrows and acquainted with grief."* Handel put music to Isaiah and Lamentations and Psalms and related the passages to Jesus. There was lots of Old Testament in Part the Second.

When I was in seminary the professors would talk about those passages. Every text must be interpreted in its historical situation, they taught. It was not good scholarship to add meanings the original author did not intend. They didn't want too much of Jesus in Isaiah. They questioned that a doctrine of Atonement should be based on Isaiah 53.

The professors did not always see clearly. Their minds had been clouded by German rationalism and the Enlightenment. My mother and Freeman and Handel, to say nothing of Matthew and the apostle Paul, saw a lot of Jesus in Isaiah, and a lot of the cross in Isaiah 53. "*Surely…Surely…*" *Largo* and *forte*. Do *Largo* and *Forte* go together?"*Surely He hath borne our griefs and carried our sorrows.*" No moral influence theory of the Atonement there.

"*And with his stripes we are healed…*"

Five pages of "*with his stripes we are healed.*"Mel Gibson did not improve on Handel, nor on the choral society. "*See if there be any sorrow like unto His sorrow…*" "*They that see him laugh him to scorn…*" "*He was cut off from the land of the living but Thou didst not leave His soul in hell…*" "*Lift up your heads, O ye gates, that the king of glory may come in.*""*Why do the nations rage so furiously together?*" (sung in 1941 on the first Saturday of December, December 6, even as the Japanese warships were descending on Pearl Harbor).

After the atonement we were then ready. Ready to stand and make the offering to God, and the witness to the world. "*Hallelujah!*" "*Hallelujah!*" "*Hallelujah!*" If they had been Pentecostals they would have lifted their hands and shouted and clapped and beat drums and jingled tambourines. Mennonites were much more somber. They stood with their somber faces. But they worshipped no less, and blessed God, and were blessed in return. For eighty-nine pages of music the great spiritual cosmic battle had taken place in Part the Second. We faced the cross, the resurrection, the ascension, and the rebellion of sin. This was the whole story as celebrated with the elders and creatures and angels and saints. We were now in heaven, in Revelation 19. "*Hallelujah.*" Double forte, for five pages. "*Hallelujah.*"

She Was A Calvinist Anyway

"She was a Calvinist anyway."

Loren said it with the same silly grin that was his trademark. Then he turned around and walked into Taylor University's Swallow-Robin dorm. I stood there dumbfounded. Over on the side, not thirty feet away, the insides of a rotten egg slid slowly down the windshield of an old Chevy. The Chevy belonged to a visiting missionary, the chapel speaker of the morning.

Loren and I both knew the egg reached the windshield quite by accident. No maliciousness was intended. Loren had aimed it down the alley where it was meant to fall harmlessly on the gravel. But Loren was a bad throw. If he had been a catcher he would have hit the water cooler in the visitor's dugout on a peg to second base. Had he aimed, he could not have hit that windshield once in a hundred tries. But having hit it, he would never admit he had not aimed for it.

But the car of a missionary? Missionaries were sanctified saints, persons who had sacrificed for Jesus, always to be treated with respect. Had it been an egg on the car of Mom Sines, our house Mother, or Jack Riggs, or anyone who lived on the third floor of Swallow-Robin, it would have been appropriate, or at least understandable. But an egg on the windshield of a kindly, somewhat inept—if the chapel address was any indication—but otherwise committed servant of Christ?

It was a tragedy, or an act of vandalism, or a reckless reflection of immaturity that is characteristic of college freshmen. It was probably a bit of each.

"She was a Calvinist anyway." That settled it. The egg throw was

SWALLOW ROBIN DORMITORY, TAYLOR UNIVERSITY, UPLAND, IND.

a justified act. At Taylor University—at least in those days—everyone was stereotyped—Calvinist or Arminian. To Loren and me—Methodist and Arminians—Calvinists were like sophomores, fine and upright sometimes, eligible to be close friends under ordinary circumstances. But under special conditions and at certain moments, sophomores and Calvinists were sometimes also irritants and nominees for justly deserved pranks, jokes, and verbal put-downs.

Actually, the missionary may or may not have been a Calvinist. But she was a friend of Mom Sines, our dorm Mother, who was one. That was close enough.

I looked at the egg, shrugged my shoulders, and followed Loren inside.

The egg had come from Bill Plumb's room, across the hall, where it had served as a dorm room knick-knack for weeks, along with dirty handkerchiefs, half-eaten oranges, unworkable pens, and other dorm room paraphernalia. Before that time it had come from the chicken who also lived in the room, not permanently but for a couple of weeks or so, after she had been discovered wandering around wet and forlorn on campus, like a freshman still in a green beanie. The chicken, who as I recall was never named—though she was, at least for a short time, a dorm pet—was showered with love and warmth, fattened by cafeteria food, and perched often on the edge of the bed or the back of a chair. Sometimes she crouched in the corner if there were too many people in the room, and it was there, on a pile of dirty clothes, that one day she presented her patrons with a big white egg. After awhile she was released somewhere near where she was found, perhaps to make her way back to some chicken coop and a flock of her friends where she could share her adventure story of life in Swallow-Robin dorm. The egg stayed on. It was I, a former chicken-raiser, who pronounced one day that it had become rotten. I knew about such things. That's when we thought it best to get rid of it.

The chicken's guest stay in Swallow-Robin was followed in the spring by the raccoons who used the Plumb-Dickey room as a nursery. Like the hen, they showed up from somewhere, presumably lost and without earthly parents or friends, two orphans, adopted into the Swallow-Robin family, where they hid out in closets and under beds and ran up and down the hall, to the obvious displeasure of Mom Sines, the dorm Mother who wasn't sure whether the boys were to be encouraged for their nurturing instincts, or reported to the dean. It was pointed out to her there was nothing in the student handbook about forbidding the housing of raccoons. The Swallow-Robin environment, with its variety of smells, sounds, and strange creatures, could not have been too unlike the woods to which they were eventually returned. The raccoons were named Cottonpicker and Potlicker. Eventually they found a home in New Jersey under the porch of a friend of Bill Plumb.

I almost did not make it to Taylor University. I believe it was an act of God, (I am enough of a Calvinist to believe God has a plan for each life). During my senior year of high school I was involved in a three-way discussion and debate that involved my father, my mother, and me, as to where I should attend college. We could agree together only that I should apply to several schools. I applied to four. My personal preferences among the four were as follows:

1) Indiana University. I had friends going there. They had a good music program (I was going to pursue music), and they had offered me a (small) music scholarship.

2) Ball State. I had friends going there. The school was good for teaching, and it was my father's first choice.

3) Wheaton College. Mother's first choice. It was known to be a

good school, difficult even to get into.

4) Taylor University. I was acquainted with it because a football gospel team had come from there to our church and I had been persuaded to fill out an application.

Mother's list of preferences was different:

1) Wheaton College. The Cadillac of the Christian schools. Berne-type people went there.

2) Taylor University. The rickshaw of the Christian schools, in case the Cadillac school did not work out.

3) Ball State. A party school to be avoided.

4) Indiana University. An even worse party school to be avoided at all costs.

My father had still a different list:

1) Ball State. They had a national guard unit and band in Muncie. Noted for teaching.

2) Indiana University. They had ROTC there, good for music.

3) Taylor. I could conceivably still be in Muncie's national guard and attend Taylor.

4) Wheaton. A school suspect if too many Berne-type people went there.

My father's case for the National Guard band won out. It was the time of the Korean War. There was a good chance I could be drafted into the army. If I joined the National Guard it would take care of my service obligations.

I joined the guard in April before I graduated from high school in May. I was excited about the prestige of the organization. This was, supposedly, not just any army unit. This was the National Guard band unit, an exceptional group consisting of some of the best musicians in the nation, or at least in central Indiana. Not just anyone could be in this unit and this band. One had to be intelligent, patriotic, and an advanced musician. It was made up of highly trained personnel, consisting in large part of Ball State students and faculty, skilled not only in music but in every area of military defense.

It was not nearly as complicated getting in as I had imagined. I remember mostly playing the scale on my trombone, having my heart listened to, and being asked if I could see the eye chart. The question about the eye chart came with some relief, since I was positive I could not fake my way through an real eye exam as I had at the license branch where I memorized the appropriate line on the eye chart ahead of time in order to pass the examination (F-E-L-O-P-Z-D—I still remember it). The light was bad at the armory and I never could have made it beyond line two.

I received my uniform and played sixth or seventh trombone. I attended band practices in April, May, and June. We went on bivouacs once. We marched in a Memorial Day parade. I held a gun.

I discovered the talents of the guard were somewhat different from what I had expected and ran somewhat in this order:

1) Drinking beer.
2) Creative cursing, outlandish story telling, and laughing wildly about stories and jokes.
3) Musical excellence.
4) Knowing how to hold a gun in case they ever needed to.

One day in June a doctor stopped by, a real-for-sure doctor. He was just checking over some of the records. He inquired about an off-hand remark on the papers from my physical. In answer to the question, "Could I hear all right?" I had responded "Yes." Then, almost as an afterthought I added, "I do not have a hole in one ear." The doctor asked about the hole in the ear, or lack of one. He looked at the non-hole, then at my eyes, and said, "You have astigmatism bad; plus you can't hear out of one ear. You can't be in the national guard. You're 4-F two times over."

I turned in my uniform and went home. Eventually I received a certificate saying I had been honorably discharged. Occasionally at a patriotic meeting where the veterans who had served in the country's armed services are asked to stand to be recognized, I stand.

Now I was back to square one on the colleges. We (I think my mother, really) called Wheaton. Sorry. I had been accepted there but when I informed them I was not coming they gave my slot to someone else. I called Indiana University. They had given my (modest) scholarship to someone else. After my guard experience I was not excited about Ball State.

So, on September 7, 1952, my mother took me to Taylor

University. I knew not a soul enrolled there. I knew it was a Christian school. I had been with the Berne-types. I figured I could fit in. My expectations were not high. It was a good thing. Taylor some years later would be ranked by *U.S. News and World Report* as the best baccalaureate college in the Midwest. But it was not anywhere near that in 1952. I was assigned to room 13 at Swallow-Robin.

I entered my room for the first time. There was no bed, nor desk, nor dresser. There was a roommate, sitting on his bed. My new roommate explained that we had to go to the warehouse and get our own beds and desks and dresser. I don't believe this is the way freshmen at colleges are greeted today. My mother was crying. I don't know if it was because she was losing her first son to college, or because of the condition of the room, or because of who my roommate was.

It didn't matter. Mothers cry.

When she left I got acquainted with Loren Lindholm, my roommate. He was from a ranch in Minnesota (good—I preferred farm kids over city kids). He was Methodist (good—I would meet enough Baptists, I was sure). One of his first questions was, "Did we have any Christian radio stations in this area?" (after he saw I had brought a radio)

"Well," I answered, "WMBI in Chicago." My mother listened to it all the time, static and all. She could barely receive the signal in LaGrange, let alone Upland. It was an unusual question to start a friendship. Actually, there were almost no Christian radio stations around in those days, and it was certainly not anywhere on my list of concerns.

Then, after a few more minutes of information sharing, Loren said, "Let's pray."

Well, I knew this was a Christian school. I wasn't sure what all that would entail, but never in my life had I met someone who asked in the first five minutes about Christian radio stations and then, "Let's pray." So we prayed.

Loren, at least initially, was much more concerned about the spiritual life of evangelicals than I was, or at least, about the appearance of spiritual life. He saw me having devotions in the evening before bed, but was convinced something was lacking if I didn't also have devotions in the morning. I told him I had never had devotions in the morning. I'm not sure how we worked that out.

My Taylor experience can be divided into two parts. Before Ruth and after Ruth. Or, the Swallow-Robin freshman year, and everything else that followed.

Taylor tried an experiment in the fall of 1952. For some reason or other, someone had the idea that the freshman boys should live all by themselves in one dorm under the supervision of a "dorm Mother" (that would be Mom Sines).

Bad decision. Mom Sines, believing that Christian boys would be well-behaved, was too nice. Putting freshman boys all together would have worked only with a drill sergeant and a whip. As it was, without Mothers, and without the moderating influence of upper classmen, and away from home, the dorm was more or less out of control. In a mild, conservative evangelical sort of way, that is. That means there were a lot of water fights.

But there was a lot more. My diary, which was still being kept faithfully at this time, records a lot of entries like "goofed off after supper," "goofed off most of the morning," or just, as a generic description of the day's activities, "goofed off." "Goofing off" was a rather general term meaning "not studying." It included bull sessions, theological debates, playing ping pong, playing basketball, telling stories about high school exploits, evaluating the freshman girls, commenting on the incompetence of professors we didn't like, and scheming against sophomores.

The not studying part was reflected in some of my freshman grades. I dutifully reported in my diary my C minuses and my F's. I got an F on an English theme (and I thought I was a good writer). Worse, I got an F on a couple of Bible projects and tests. One F came after I was gone for several days for 4-H Club Congress, a trip I had won earlier. I knew I had a Bible test but figured with all my years of Bible school and reading the Bible I would know enough answers for a respectable grade. I failed to take into account that Professor Thompson had said the test would be over material in the text and the material in the text was about the mystery religions. I had never even heard of mystery religions. I had incorrectly assumed that at a Christian school a Bible test would be over the Bible.

The scheming against the sophomores was much easier since all the freshmen boys, and only freshmen boys, were in one dorm. Sophomores, on the other hand, were in Wisconsin dorm, mixed in with upper classmen. They were not organized. They did not naturally congregate in the rest rooms to scheme.

The ringleader for the freshmen was Bill Plumb. Bill was eight years older than the rest of us. He had fought in Korea. Those were enough credentials to get him elected class president at one of the earliest freshman meetings. My first impression of Bill was that he was too old and was probably much too mature to be of much fun. It was a mis-impression. He was neither too old nor too mature. It was Bill who plotted stealing the sophomore class sweaters before they were formally presented to the class on class day in the fall.

The freshmen found out that the sweaters were being hid at the class sponsor's house. So, on Sports Day, during the bicycle race (won by the freshmen which did not endear our class to the others), a delegation hurriedly arrived at the sponsor's house and announced breathlessly to the sponsor's wife that the freshmen had found out where the sweaters were being hidden and were on their way to steal them and this group had come to move them and re-hide them and keep them safe.

The ploy worked. That's how we got the sweaters. Keeping the sweaters was more complicated. The sophomores came to retrieve the sweaters, by force if necessary. If they couldn't get the sweaters they would get the class president, Bill Plumb. They couldn't find him. Bill was hiding out in the prayer chapel (even at a Christian college the prayer chapel was not thought of as a hiding place). Eventually they kidnapped him from his room when he was in pajamas, and threatened torture if he did not produce the sweaters. When he did not, they blindfolded him took him on a country road and dumped him out.

When that didn't work they stormed Swallow-Robin dorm. But it had been barricaded and was being defended with buckets of water. When it appeared that the sophomores were gaining entry Ken

Gangel jumped from the 3rd floor balcony to defend the freshman honor. This is the same Ken Gangel who would later become academic dean of Dallas Theological Seminary, author of 57 books, lecturer at 40 different educational institutions and considered one of the most influential Christian educators of the 20th century. But in 1952 Gangel was just a silly freshman. Gangel broke his ankle. The sophomores had some pity and took him to the hospital, but not before they shaved his head. Bill Plumb was captured and also got shaved. But the secret of the sweaters was not revealed and the sophomores had nothing to present at class day, to the great glee of the freshmen. We acclaimed our freshman year as a success.

That some of the same rowdy boys of the freshman dorm would one day become ministers, teachers, doctors, and successful businessmen and Christian leaders is one of the mysteries of the faith. It is also one of the reasons for the existence of Christian schools. I was certainly never intending to end up being a minister when I entered Taylor. I was comfortable with my casual evangelical faith, helped put in place by Mother and her relatives, Methodist church camp, and summer Bible school, but I had no special interest in moving it from the periphery of my life to the center.

That slowly changed. First, there were the prayer meetings. Taylor delighted in prayer meetings. We had all-school prayer meetings, class prayer meetings, choir prayer meetings, dorm prayer meetings, and dorm floor prayer meetings. I can't remember what we prayed for at all of those prayer meetings. I believe we prayed for the spiritual health of the campus and for some among us who were lukewarm in the faith.

Then we had bull sessions (long talks in the night). Bull sessions were about every conceivable topic: the advantages or disadvantages of small town living; whether the Methodist Church was apostate; whether it was better to have graduated from a small high school or a large high school; whether Indiana or Ohio was a better state. One time the topic was whether Swallow Robin Hall was really a nut house that our parents had sent us to to get us out of the house.

Sometimes, actually quite often, bull sessions were debates, quite often about things related to being Calvinist or Arminian.

The favorite topic was Eternal Security. Our house Mother, Mom Sines, was a participant in these debates. I have a memory of her prowling around the halls with Bible open, ready to defend the perseverance of the saints. One time, upon hearing a debate in one of the rooms Mom Sines charged in unannounced, ready for battle. She was already on her third point when someone mentioned to her that, in case she had not noticed, we were all in our underwear. We weren't always motivated to read the Bible for Prof Thompson's New Testament 101 but we were motivated to read the Bible to find new texts for the next Calvinist-Arminian skirmish.

My freshman year was also about music. I was planning on a career in music. I sometimes tell people (later) that I was convinced I could save the world with my trombone. To further this goal I was taking trombone lessons and played in Taylor's trombone quartet. Our quartet's most notable contribution to Taylor life was to climb to the top of the Administration Building and play Bach chorales on the tower platform during the Bach Festival, a Taylor event designed to introduce culture to otherwise culturally-deprived Taylor students. I heard some years later that the highest consistent wind velocity in Indiana is at a certain altitude above Upland, Indiana. Since the Administration Building was the highest point in Upland we already knew by experience the highest wind velocity in Indiana was above Upland, Indiana, or, more specifically, at the small platform on top of the Administration Building. Our trombone sounds probably never made it to the ground but they may have been heard in Hartford City, seven miles away. However, we hung on to the railing around the open platform, were not blown off, and lived for another day.

I also played trombone-trumpet duets with my friend Norm Wingert. Our contribution to saving the world was a fair rendition of "When They Ring Them Golden Bells" played at several nearby country churches during revival services. Norm was also my ping-pong partner. A year later when I was at Northwestern University, Norm hitch-hiked to visit me for the weekend. The only possessions he brought along were his ping-pong paddle, his trumpet, and his tooth brush. He said he traveled light with only the essentials.

Norm was also a part of our freshman gospel quartet, along with

John Terrell, and Bill Plumb, and me. According to my diary we sang on thirty different occasions during March, April, and May, 1953. This was in the days when we thought we were too sophisticated for southern gospel, but we did do, whenever we thought we could get away with it, a wild rendition of "Gospel Boogie."

In A Cappella choir some of the students debated with Prof Pearson over how much gospel music to incorporate into concerts. The argument was that a little Latin music was all right for sophisticated audiences (although we never sang much for sophisticated audiences); but the churches we sang in were more responsive to gospel music. When Prof relented and allowed us to sing "Great Is Thy Faithfulness" it became one of my favorite hymns, and later a favorite for our family.

I believe we were singing "Great Is Thy Faithfulness" one night late coming home from a concert in Cincinnati. We often sang in the bus. It was at that point things started to come together. I suggested to a couple of friends that we spend time in the prayer chapel when we got home. Later I would testify that we prayed much of the night. I was corrected by my diary with this entry:

When home Bill Plumb, Norm, Loren, and I prayed for 2 hours until we got victory. I was wonderful.

"Victory" was the word we used to mean "sanctification," or "new spiritual life" (if one was a Calvinist). I look back on it as a turning point in my life. I told the Lord I was ready for whatever He had for me. I was not thinking about the ministry at that point but one should not give God a blank check. The next year I would meet Ruth, be called to the ministry, meet new friends, and—perhaps not least—start studying.

The Ring Was In The Pocket

September 3, 1955, a day I had long been looking forward to. It was 7:00 AM and I was standing along U.S. 75 outside the city limits of Ortonville, Minnesota. It was my intent to hitchhike the 290 miles or so to Mandan, North Dakota, there to see my girl-friend— actually, my soon-to-be fiancé. You see, the ring was in the pocket.

That would be the engagement ring, purchased several days before at Thurston Jewelers, Minneapolis. I am not exactly sure why, now years later, the ring had to be

Ruth and Riley on Taylor campus, 1955

purchased at Thurstones. It was, no doubt, because my friend and college roommate, Loren Lindholm, had purchased his ring for Tuckie there and had offered a reason for buying a ring there that sounded good to me. Mr. Swanson was a Christian, a member of the Covenant Church, and would give a good deal. I was suspicious of jewelers, so Thurstones was the place.

It had been a long summer. Loren spent it with me in LaGrange. Both he and I started out the summer with high expectations. The Indiana toll road was being built; the toll road needed workers;

they paid good wages. Loren was wanting something different from going back to Ortonville, to his father's ranch, to bale hay and pitch manure. He could stay with me, earn money, and we would have a good time together.

I had made the contact. I was interested in a job on the toll road. Would companies be hiring? It was a phone call. The answer was yes. We were to show up at a certain date at a certain place. I took that to mean we were hired. I told friends and family my summer would be spent working on the toll road.

I was young and naïve. Loren and I went to our first day of work only to discover that the word that companies were hiring did not necessarily mean that we were hired. Yes they were hiring but there were many more job-seekers than there were jobs. The first question asked was, "Did we belong to the union?" We did not. Union people were hired. We were not.

It was a depressing day. Not only did I not have a job, I now had to explain why I did not have a job, which was, that I had misread the situation badly. Not only that, but I had misled my friend Loren. He was committed to stay at my parent's home all summer. He would be better off at home baling hay (though he was not certain of that).

Eventually we both got jobs at Walter's foundry outside LaGrange. The pay was $1.25 an hour, not nearly as good as $3.50 an hour on the toll road, but it was a job. The foundry was making aluminum light guards. It employed six or eight persons. As the summer wore on 6 or 8 became five, then, three, and then only Loren and me. On the positive side, I was learning something about foundries (which would never do me a bit of good in life). I learned how to make molds, pour hot aluminum, and grind off the rough edges of the guards. The enterprise was not going well. Mr. Walters was using recycled aluminum which meant our aluminum was not high quality, which meant that the light guards were cracking.

One day Mr. Walters told us how much he was getting per light guard. I did the math. He was losing money. The whole operation was a disaster in the making and there was nothing we could do about it. Our plan had been to quit ten days before we had to be back at Taylor University. We would drive Loren's car to his home in

Ortonville. From there I would go on to North Dakota to visit Ruth, then come back to Minnesota and with Loren return to Indiana for school.

We quit a week early. They say that absence makes the heart grow fonder. Loren had been absent from Tuckie (back in Ortonville), his betrothed, all summer, and his heart was fond. My heart was fond also, although I knew I could not show up at the Unkenholz farm early and expect to stay an extra week. Plus I felt some guilt about leaving Mr. Walters and his sinking ship. I apologized when I told him we wanted to leave early. He seemed relieved (a short time later the foundry closed).

So we left for Minnesota. I could spend time in Minneapolis with my other roommate, Ray Isley, and time in Ortonville with Loren. The time in Minneapolis allowed me to get the ring. In Ortonville I helped Loren bale hay and pitch manure. Loren's father was not the kind to allow a son to be unproductive even with company. This meant if I stayed I should help. I didn't mind. Baling hay and pitching manure. The ring was in the pocket. On Saturday I would start out for North Dakota.

The day was beautiful, that Saturday morning, September 3rd on route 75 heading north to Fargo. I recall a euphoric feeling. I was going to see my Ruth. Before the day was over I would give her kisses. Her parents and family were, I was sure, wonderful. Ruth had always told me that, and today I would find out. I would be in North Dakota. I would see the sky she spoke of, and the stars, and the clouds. Some states boast of mountains; others of lakes; others of seashore; others of forests; North Dakota boasts of clouds. While clouds are in all states they are supposed to be special in North Dakota.

I didn't mind the thought of hitchhiking. It was an adventure. I had done it before. I had no anxieties that I would not get rides. I soon got my first ride but it was only for 20 miles or so. People on highway 75 in Minnesota are not traveling cross country; they tend rather to be going only to the next town. I got another ride to another town, and then another. I made it to Fargo, and then had to walk to get to a better hitch-hiking spot. My big suitcase was not designed for walking. Then a ride came that was going all the way to Bismarck. On U.S. 10 people would be going farther than the next town. They would be on their way to Oregon, or at least Bismarck. The driver entertained me (and himself) with talk of his football career at the University of Texas where Bobby Lane (the famous quarterback—at least famous at that time) was his roommate. Somewhere along U.S. 10 we stopped and ate. Somewhere else along U.S. 10 the car developed problems. The Bobby Lane guy asked me if I wanted out or wanted to wait while he stopped to have someone work on the car. I waited.

North Dakota was green. It was not always so. There had been and would be dry years, dusty years, hot years in the summer, brown years. But this year it was green. Ten miles out of Fargo and I loved it already.

Sometime around 3:00 we made it to Bismarck. 280 miles in 8 hours. Not bad. Ruth had said a good place to wait was the Patterson Hotel on U.S. 10. I called her number at the farm. Ruth was expecting the call. She would be coming in. I could sense the kisses. The ring was in the pocket.

Ruth told me over the phone the threshing crews were there. I didn't catch the significance of that. I had only thoughts for the kisses. My heart was fond.

It was a long wait. Ten hours or so, though Ruth claims it was less than an hour. Thirty years later I would have made a sarcastic remark but not then. Her comment about coming right in really meant right away after she had had a bath and changed clothes and fixed herself up. As far as I was concerned she didn't need a bath and she didn't need to fix herself up. I just wanted her. After all, it had been three months. Three months in days before cell phones and email. No way to communicate except by letter.

The wait at the Patterson Hotel gave me time to reflect. It was almost two years before, almost the very date, that we met at Taylor. She was an answer to prayer, though she didn't know it at the time. I have no idea why, at the tender age of 20, I believed it was time for me to get serious about marriage and a future; but I did. I was tired of the girls at LaGrange. I believe it was pure prejudice. My mother's skepticism about the spiritual life of LaGrange had rubbed off on me. There were but few Christians in LaGrange, I was led to believe. If a young man wanted a girl he could spend his life with he needed to go to Berne, Mother's home town, or a Christian college. But there was some truth in the prejudice. The girls I had known had been fun, and I liked them all, but I could not see myself spending my life with any of them. A year at Taylor had convinced me I really wanted someone "spiritual," a strong Christian. Of course I wanted lots of other things too—good-looking, sexy, smart, fun to be with—and of course she needed to play the piano. I was still believing I was God's gift to the world on the trombone, but I needed someone who not only enjoyed music but could accompany me on the trombone (which sounds extremely self-centered today).

A few days before returning to Taylor for my sophomore year I prayed about it. I normally was not one to pray about such things as girlfriends (I figured I could do that on my own without any special divine intervention) but I was momentarily despondent. I was home from a date in LaGrange. It was late at night. I was in the bathroom. I was soon returning to Taylor. I knew (most of) the girls who had been in my freshmen class at Taylor. I was intimidated by some of them, and not excited about the ones I was not intimidated by. I believe the girls I was intimidated by were from cities. I assumed they knew more, had more experience, and would see me as backward. Actually, I did not personify self-confidence.

Whatever. I prayed. Lord, lead me to someone I can love and get serious with—or something like that. Whatever the words, it was a specific prayer well remembered.

Four days later Ruth walked through the door at MaGee-Campbell. I had prayed to God to find a girl but I was not above helping God along with the search. Taylor had asked for volunteers to come to school early and help incoming students with luggage. We were bell-boys or something like that. I was ready. I volunteered. I came early. I hauled a lot of suitcases and lamps and pillows, especially in the girls' dorm and especially with an eye for prospects.

That's when Ruth walked through the door. Someone identified her. She was Marion Unkenholz's sister. Of course that wasn't any help since I didn't know Marion Unkenholz (Ruth's sister who had been at Taylor for two years but had transferred to nurse's training). But it marked her. I made a mental note. Follow up on Marion Unkenholz's sister. Actually, for the first two months at Taylor Ruth was known primarily as Marion Unkenholz's sister, or Dick Unkenholz's sister (her brother had graduated from Taylor). Eventually, she got her own identity.

The student council met. I was representing the sophomore class. The council had a special responsibility. The incoming freshman class did not know each other and would not be able to select their own representatives to the student council. The present council would appoint the freshman representatives. To help us in the task we would arrange for members of the student council to escort the persons we identified as prospects, to the student-faculty reception. Upper-class boys escorted freshman girls and upper-class girls escorted freshman boys. The pairings were more or less at random except for the secret pre-arranged pairings.

The council identified the prospects. Rosie Baugh mentioned Ruth. Of course Rosie was a friend of Marion Unkenholz; so Ruth had an advantage over others. I non-chalantly indicated I would do my student council duty and escort the Unkenholz girl. To help us know better who we were escorting the council had prearranged that we should have access to the student college applications. It was then I began to suspect I had hit pay dirt.

Ruth Unkenholz, Mandan, North Dakota. Methodist. Valedictorian. Interests: plays piano, reads. Had accompanied her high school choir. Grew up on a farm. Accepted Christ at Washburn camp. All that sounded good to me.

So we went to the student-faculty reception. I was assuming that Ruth, innocent freshman, believing that I was a random choice, knew nothing about me. I assumed wrong. Her sister Marion, knowing how things worked, saw my picture in the Taylor annual and remarked, "You'll probably go to the student-faculty reception with him." In addition, Ruth had read a *Farm Journal* article in which I had been a panelist at a 4-H round-up and was expounding on dating.

So she was assuming I knew nothing about her. I was assuming she knew nothing about me. The person who really did know nothing about either of us was another freshman girl. Since there were more boys than girls our couple was actually a threesome.

I was hardly the big man on campus at the reception. No chance there to impress this freshman girl from North Dakota. Most of the faculty members I was supposed to be introducing the freshman girls to had no idea who I was. But they did know about Marion Unkenholz, Ruth's sister, and Dick Unkenholz, Ruth's brother. So most of the faculty small talk was about where Marion and Dick were now and what were they doing.

After the reception I asked Ruth if she would like to take a walk Sunday afternoon. She did. I talked. I talked way too much (as she later related), mostly about myself.

From there on there was a weeding out process. She tried dating some other guys. I was checking out other freshman girls, but eventually it was narrowed down to her and me. I finally took her to Berne to meet the aunts. I introduced her as Ruth Unkenholz; my Aunt Eva later asked, "And how do you spell your name?" Ruth replied, "R-U-T-H."

My mother was pleased when she met Ruth. Sensible girl. Knew how to cook. Played the piano. A Methodist, but that did not mean she would be that all her life. My father must have had some opinion but I don't know what it was.

Ruth was intriguing. She grew up in North Dakota miles from anywhere. For a few of her growing up years her family was without electricity and indoor plumbing. She went eight grades to a one-room school, where at least for several years, she was the only student in her grade. She walked a mile to the school including in the winter when the temperature could get to 20 below. For high school she boarded in town and with her brother and sister and did her own housekeeping. I believe she thought it was a plain, boring life, but I saw her as a frontier pioneer.

She loved the Lord. I grew spiritually. Ruth and I would go to the prayer chapel after the evening meal. I began studying. It actually did occur to me (this is not just a story) that Ruth would be an ideal pastor's wife. Therefore, maybe I should consider a call to the ministry. By November I was ready to change my major from music to psychology.

Somewhere in the process I (or we) began thinking of marriage, and even talked about it, usually quite generally. We would casually look at rings and she would point out the kind of ring she liked. Marriage, though, would have to be after she graduated (1957).

I reasoned backwards. If we married in June of 1957 when would it be appropriate to be engaged? Maybe a year and a half before that (November, 1955). So in that early September, 1955, I was ready. I had saved up my money. I was in the city where the rings were (Minneapolis). I bought the ring so that when I went to see her parents for the first time, the ring was in the pocket.

Ruth finally showed up at the Patterson Hotel in Bismarck. Time for kisses? No. Well, maybe one little kiss as a greeting. To a bystander there was no indication that this was a big occasion, that the ring was in the pocket. Nonetheless, she looked fantastic. Tanned, hair bleached lighter. She had sent me a photo during the summer. She had worked at Camp Grassick, a camp for handicapped children. She was in shorts in the photo with a bit of leg showing. Not much leg but in those days we were happy for what we could get.

I was hoping we could find a secluded spot and have a proper greeting. She indicated we ought to see her sister Marion, in the dorm at Nursing School in Bismarck. Marion was not there but we saw two of Ruth's high school friends. Then we had to stop at the grocery store. When you live 16 miles from the nearest store you always stop at the store. It made sense but I was wondering why we were not heading for the farm. The reason was—threshing. I didn't catch the implications of that until we pulled into the drive. There were cars all around. There were people. I was obviously not the main show on that day. This was not conducive for kisses.

But, I thought; it is near the end of the day. The people will soon be gone.

Wrong. It was 4:30 or so. Threshing keeps going until the job is done, or it is too dark to see, whichever comes first. This was North Dakota, at the western end of the time zone. Even in September it did not get dark until 9:00. The threshing day was only half over.

"You can help." That was Ruth's idea of entertaining me. Panic. I began thinking back over what I had told Ruth about my being a farm boy. I believe I had overstated my case. I actually lived in town and raised chickens. I had never pitched shocks of wheat on a wagon. I had never driven a team of horses.

But of course I would help. Gulp. Clothes were found. Farm clothes. A long-sleeved shirt (real farmers never wore short-sleeved shirts in those days), gloves, a straw hat, jeans (which we called overalls). And a pitchfork.

My fears were unfounded. No one expected me to know much, or work hard. I was assigned to Ruth's father, Grant, who was at his gracious best. He shared the love of his life, the farm. His grandfather William had come to North Dakota 75 years before and homesteaded. His son, Sam, Grant's father, worked the homestead but also looked over land for his own homestead. He was the one who picked the spot where the farm—called Ridgeview—now stood. The other settlers from the East, from Indiana, Illinois, and Iowa, had picked the flat land where it would be easier to farm. What they did not know was that the land was flat because alkaline pools once stood there. The land grew nothing. The land was hilly. The valleys were called coulees. They collected snow in the winter and thus could grow grass (and wheat) in a very dry climate.

The wheat had been planted around the coulees. That, he explained, was why they still used horses and threshed. Not enough big fields to use combines.

What a wonderful way to get acquainted. He listened to me tell about raising chickens and being in 4-H. We never would have had this conversation in a living room or around a table. But there, pitching shocks of wheat, it was natural.

Grant introduced me to all the other help. Ruth's brother Jim was helping. As were Willard and Bob and Ruth's Uncle Bill, and Merlin, and others whose names now I have forgotten. These were the people that would become family. Unknown to me at that time, this visit to the farm was only the first of 50 more to come. I would roam those coulees (especially later when I became a bird-watcher) and know the land better than the farm in LaGrange County for which I would eventually become responsible.

The first question nearly everyone asked was, "Had I ever threshed before?" I started out by telling of helping thresh a few years before when my father still threshed. Actually, it had been many years before, when I was about seven, and what I did was carry a water jar on a wagon. I toned down my story.

Suddenly I was euphoric again. These were great people; this was great place; I felt like a real farm guy. Ruth and I would soon be together alone. And the ring was in the pocket.

It was nearly dark when we finished. I had a bath. Ruth's mother fixed a great supper, mostly, as I recall, what was left-over from the big threshers' meal earlier.

Finally, it was time for the walk. The stars were wondrous to behold, just like Ruth had explained many times. They filled the sky in a way I had never seen in Indiana with haze and competing lights and obscuring trees. There was still enough moon to light the way through the farmyard.

When we got to the chicken coop we paused and I got my kisses. Wonderful kisses, in the moonlight with the smell of the just-threshed straw (plus the chicken coop smell which I didn't mind at all—I was after all, the chicken expert). And we talked about how me missed each other and what a great year we would have.

And the ring was in the pocket.

Of course, there would be more than one version of that memorable day, September 3, 1955. Ruth, after all, kept a diary. The following is her complete and unabridged record of the day:

Saturday, September 3, 1955
Grace came over to help us cook for threshers. Carol came over and swapped in the afternoon. Riley B. phoned about 3 & I went in and got him

at the Patterson in Bis. We drove around a little. Didn't see Marion but did see Judy & Curtis. Mom went with us to the church to see Carol's slides after.

But then again, she didn't know the ring was in the pocket. (I gave the ring nearly 3 months later, over the Thanksgiving break.)

Wedding day, June 28, 1957. Ruth and Riley

Nothing Among You
Save Jesus Christ

I was looking at a Holstein cow. There were three cows, as I
remember. I am not sure what the other two were but I remember
one was a Holstein. Three cows in a field on a gravel road in rural
Adams County. The cows weren't supposed to be there. I looked
again at my directions. There was supposed to be a church there,
Union Chapel Methodist Church, where I was the newly appointed
pastor. Sunday, October 14, 1956. I had it on the authority of the
district superintendent of the Fort Wayne District, Dr. Byron Stroh.
I looked again at my directions. This was before I knew that district
superintendents were not infallible.

No panic for the moment, but some concern. I was lost, in
the middle of Adams County, Indiana, on gravel roads far from
anywhere. At the time when I should have been selecting the first
hymn for the first service of my first church, I was lost.

The appointment was only several days old. The churches of
the circuit had indicated that they had been without a pastor long
enough and if the district superintendent did not intend to appoint
a pastor they would find one themselves. In fact, they had someone
all picked out. Some independent pastor was looking for a pulpit. If
you ever want to get a district superintendent's attention, mention an
independent pastor ready to come in and take over a church.

The call had come like an SOS. Did I still want a church? I was
twenty-two years old, looking seventeen. Unmarried but with a wife
promised. At the time of the call I had exactly one day of seminary.
But I was ready. College had prepared me with two years of Greek,

a hodge-podge of notes on the sermons of chapel speakers, and the ability to triple-tongue on the trombone. But more importantly, I was eager, and called of God.

The Lord had spoken to me as a freshman at Taylor University. He chased me around campus a while until I finally said, "OK, Lord, I'm ready for whatever you have in mind for me" (that's a short version of a two-hour prayer meeting). When I said OK I assumed the Lord and I both knew that would not include the ministry.

I assumed wrong. The Lord spoke to me about that nearly a year later. In the meantime I had met Ruth. She could play the piano, or rather, she could accompany me on the trombone; we would make a great team. She talked about the will of God, and I got all concerned about the will of God. About that time the Lord said, "Now, about the ministry…." I should have known it is a dangerous thing to give God a blank check. So I said yes. Not easily of course. It's a long story but in the end I was sure. I was called and anointed and elected and set aside and sent: to proclaim the unsearchable riches of Jesus Christ; to pray down heaven; to conquer kingdoms, to quench raging fires, open up the treasures of the Greek verbs in the New Testament; to reduce congregations to tears through the playing "Sound the Battle Cry" on my trombone.

That call gave me a tremendous sense of purpose. I discovered studying. Books, which had been enemies, became friends. I finished work on a license to preach. I debated agnostics. I argued denominations and seminaries. I re-fought the fundamentalist-modernist controversy. I worked out variations on "Sound the Battle Cry" on the trombone. Ruth and I talked about life together in the ministry.

Thus I was ready when the call came. Dr. Stroh, the district superintendent asked, "Did I know where Geneva was?"

Did I know? It was only a few miles from Berne where Mother grew up, where my aunts lived and my cousins. Geneva Circuit had three churches and was considered a full-time appointment. I didn't panic until a few days later when people at seminary told me seminary was a full-time job. I would now have two full-time jobs, 240 miles apart. The churches were very conservative, according to the district superintendent (that was for my benefit, I am sure; my reputation was established before I ever preached my first sermon). They would have revival meetings and prayer meetings (great, just what I wanted, none of this liberal stuff for me).

The previous pastor had a heart attack three months before and it was now determined he would not be able to return. However, according to Dr. Stroh, there would be problems. Distance for one. Geneva was 240 miles from seminary where I was full-time. The churches would not be happy with a student. He looked at me but didn't say it: especially a 22-year old looking 17. It was not good that I would not be present for mid-week prayer meetings.

The salary would be $3,000. That was a jolt. It was more than I had ever dreamed of. It sounded like a million dollars. At our first meeting the superintendent indicated it was only a possibility. I shared the news with Ruth. She was senior at Taylor. We were excited.

Ten days later the call came to go. Go immediately. Go this coming Sunday. I was at seminary 240 miles away until Friday. No time for Pastor Parish Committees; no time for interviews; no time to drive by the church or the parsonage. An independent preacher was waiting in the wings. Revival meetings were two weeks away at Union Chapel. There could be trouble. I knew nothing about trouble. All I heard was, "Go."

My sermon was already picked out. It was a message from God: I Corinthians 2:2, "For I determined to know nothing among you save Jesus Christ and him crucified." I had worked on that sermon for six months, in preparation for this day. The idea had come from E. Stanley Jones. In March, back in carefree days, Ruth and I had gone to Florida with friends for spring break. There, away from the pressure of school, with orange blossoms and my fiancée in a spring dress (some things you don't forget) I read *Christ of the Indian Road* by E. Stanley Jones. I had picked this book out particularly because it happened to be sitting on my desk when I thought about taking a book. It was available. It was also small and fit into my suitcase. Otherwise I would not have taken it. I was suspicious of E. Stanley Jones. Testimonies of his greatness were mingled with rumors that he was a socialist and a liberal. Furthermore, the book was 30 years old and I had picked up some snobbishness that anything before World War II must be irrelevant.

The book was a God-sent blessing. I became an E. Stanley Jones fan. And I knew I had not only my first sermon for my first church, but a philosophy for my ministry. According to E. Stanley Jones, our only message is Jesus Christ and him crucified. We do not preach the church, nor Americanism, nor religion, nor just being good, nor culture; we don't even preach Christianity. We preach Jesus. Nothing but Jesus.

I worked on that sermon all summer. I was at home that summer, in LaGrange, with a job in Sturgis, Michigan. I was preaching that sermon in the chicken coop when a squadron of bees flew in and attacked me. Opposition to the gospel it must be, but I would not be derailed; my course was set. Nothing but Jesus.

That sermon was there on October 14, 1956, in my Bible, my big, black Bible. I had very little experience or training about what preachers said and did or how they looked; but I knew a preacher was supposed to carry a big, black Bible. The day before, Saturday, I stayed in Berne with Uncle Wilbur and Aunt Selma. Ruth came early Sunday morning. Family devotions at breakfast had changed little since I had stayed with Uncle Wilbur as a child. The devotions were special on that day. Uncle Wilbur prayed especially for me, for the anointing of the Holy Spirit, for strength and guidance, and for souls. It was like a commissioning service.

With that kind of send-off I could not possibly fail. I was the apostle Paul leaving Antioch. I was David Livingston plunging into Africa, with the message, "nothing but Jesus."

But of course it would be helpful to know one additional thing besides Jesus, and that was, where was the church? Well, we left the Holstein and retraced our steps. We knew of no one to call and we had no access to a phone anyway. We stopped at a farmhouse. No one home. Another farmhouse. No one home. Of course. People were all religious in Adams County. Everybody was in church. Well, not exactly everybody. We finally found someone at home; but they had never heard of Union Chapel. Now I began to get worried. What would Billy Graham do in a situation like this? Finally we found a house that had a person that knew where the church was. A mile or so this way, a mile that way. Finally, we arrived. A beautiful, country church, brick. A row of cars--no welcoming committee, but a row of cars.

Now what? It was right in the middle of Sunday school. We walked up the steps of that beautiful church. I opened the door--and let Ruth go in first. No one was in the vestibule. What are you supposed to do when you arrive at your first church and don't know a single person? Not the lay leader, not the Sunday school superintendent, not the organist. Actually, the pianist, since there was no organ.

I tried the door to the sanctuary--and let Ruth go in first. Two classes were meeting in the sanctuary, one on either side. We looked at the class nearest us. They looked back out of the corner of their eyes and through the back of their heads. The teacher was expounding on the kings of Israel. He looked at us while he expounded about Zedekiah or whoever and never missed a beat. The class on the far side was interested by this time. One thing was sure—people in country churches so far away they cannot even be found, are not used to strangers.

I decided on a strategy. Taking Ruth in tow I left the sanctuary and went to the basement. I found the class with the smallest children and I introduced myself. I was the new pastor and I was sorry we were late but we got lost. It didn't matter one way or the other to the 3-year olds, but the teacher was impressed. From there I moved to the class with elementary children, repeated the process, then to the youth class.

Then I tried upstairs again. My confidence was increasing by this time. On a scale of 1 to 10 it had risen from 1 to 2. With this entrance we upstaged the kings of Israel. Whatever point the teacher was making was surely lost because now the class gave me its undivided attention. So I spoke: "Hi, my name is Riley Case, I am your new preacher. This is my fiancée Ruth Unkenholz. We intended to get here earlier, but we got lost."

A few years later I could have expanded that into a 10-minute speech but I had not yet learned to be pompous, and I didn't know much else to say; after all, I was determined to know nothing save Jesus Christ.

There was a curious silence, as if everyone was trying to figure out something appropriate to say in return. After no one figured anything to say, and without comment, the teacher went back to the kings of Israel. Ruth and I sat down near the class—a part of it and yet not quite a part of it—to ponder out next move.

We weren't the only ones pondering. For all of its efficiency the Methodist system sometimes breaks down. The Lord, the district superintendent, Ruth, Uncle Wilbur, and I all knew I had been appointed as pastor of Union Chapel Methodist Church, but Union Chapel Methodist Church people didn't know it. There was a miscommunication, or perhaps more accurate, a non-communication. The people in that country church had not the slightest idea who I was or where I had come from. It is not every Sunday that some twenty-two year old kid walks into a discussion on the kings of Israel and announces he had been sent by God to be their new pastor.

That such a situation like this could even exist is only conceivable in the Methodist system. Baptists and Lutherans have problems, but not of this variety. Most churches call their ministers. Candidates preach trial sermons; they are examined, reviewed, and voted on. But Methodists are sent and Union Chapel had just become painfully aware of that, in a way not quite intended.

And I, for all of my expertise on the trombone and my knowledge of Greek verbs, was totally naïve. I was determined to know nothing but Jesus, and that is exactly what I knew. I knew Jesus, but little else. I had not the slightest clue that I was unexpected. I had missed every sign that something was not quite right. The church, for its part, was doing its best to cope. They did not want to be seen as not even knowing the new pastor was coming, so they were covering up, sort of.

They were huddled, the leaders among them, over in the corner, trying to figure out what to do.

Glen Dale came up, good old Glen Dale. I visited with him in 2009 (53 years later); he remembers nothing about that Sunday; I guess it was just another day for him. At the time he did what needed to be done. Glen Dale was song leader, worship leader, master of ceremonies, whatever. He introduced himself, asked what I had planned. He normally was the song leader but he would be happy if I would take charge of the entire service; whatever I said.

It suddenly occurred to me that I knew nothing but Jesus, and I had nothing planned. I had not been concerned about bulletins. I had not looked up any hymns. I knew nothing about how one took up the offering. I yielded graciously to Glen Dale. I would be pleased if he would handle the service. We agreed I would give the prayer, take up the offering, preach, and he would do the rest.

But I was not yet home free. Another special person was there: Fred Bushy, from Decatur, the district lay leader. District lay leaders normally do not have a lot to do, but when they do do something, it can be important. The district lay leader represents the district superintendent, and the conference, and the denomination. Fred was at Union Chapel on that day because he was, first of all, the scheduled preacher for the morning. But he also was there because he was under orders from the district superintendent. He was a person with authority. Fred was supposed to keep an eye on things at Union Chapel, especially since there was some independent preacher that might be coming in to take over. If this independent pastor moved in Fred would defend the district superintendent, the *Discipline*, the Methodist Church, the kingdom, and the Lord (in whatever order) against all ecclesiastical irregularities.

He appeared the moment the closing Sunday school exercise benediction had been given. He tugged at my coat. "Come over here. I would like a word with you." We moved over under a stained glass window. He asked a very direct question.

"Who sent you?"

It was a question ready-made to warm the heart of any man called by God. After three-years preparation, hours in the prayer chapel with Ruth as we planned our life together, after learning all about the aorist tense in Greek, filled with knowledge all country churches ought to have, after learning hymn variations to be played on the trombone, now the moment had arrived. I was invited to give witness to my calling.

"Who sent me?"

What an opening for a witness to my calling:"God sent me, the triune God—Father, Son, and Holy Spirit. The Lord of the heavens. The God who raised Jesus from the dead. King of Kings. He said to me, 'Go, and preach the gospel.'"

That would have been the wrong response. At that moment I did recall the d.s. had mentioned some independent preacher. To this day I am not convinced there ever was an independent preacher. No matter. I needed to give an appropriate response. I thank God for the Holy Spirit who gives wisdom.

"The district superintendent sent me."God would have his chance later on.

"What is his name?" Did every new pastor go through a test like this?

"Byron Stroh." Fred's face relaxed somewhat. Never underestimate the power of the name of the district superintendent in the Methodist Church.

"When did you talk with him?" The questioning continued but the pressure was off.

"Monday."

The district lay leader was persuaded my preaching would not endanger God's kingdom.

By this time the piano prelude was nearly over. I took my seat and prayed. One of the matters I worried about months previous was whether I was supposed to kneel by the pulpit chair to pray before the service. I saw someone do that once. My mind was on matters of lesser importance. The song service began:

I heard an old, old story, of a savior came from glory.

I remember the songs we sang at Union Chapel. To tell the truth, I had never heard "Victory in Jesus" before I heard it at Union Chapel church. We didn't even sing it at Taylor University. Those songs are old friends to me know. The people loved them. More singing, along with running exhortations by Glen Dale.

The order of service was singing, praying, offering, preaching. No responsive reading, no Gloria Patri, no prayers read from a bulletin. No bulletin.

It was sermon time. I told a bad joke. Along with carrying a big, black Bible, I thought preachers needed to start with a joke. Strangers don't tell jokes well. I don't think I ever started a sermon with a joke after that.

I gave my message: "I determined to know nothing among you save Jesus Christ and him crucified." It was, by that time, a nearly memorized oration, done with great seriousness. Had it been preached by Billy Graham it would not have been with any more prayer and urgency. I was encouraged with an "Amen" and another, and a "that's right" or two. Rural Methodism was not dead.

It was great. Fifteen minutes, no more. In two more months I would hit 16 minutes, within six months I could do 17 minutes. Years later I went back to the circuit. One man told me I was the best preacher they ever had. Pride. Then he explained, "You always stopped after 15 minutes." I've preached "nothing but Jesus" as the first sermon at every new church I've been appointed to. I looked it up in my sermon file. Every time I preached it I revised it. The last time I preached it it lasted 33 minutes.

When the service was over the pressure was off. People were laughing and talking, introducing themselves. You didn't stand at the door and welcome people as they went out at Union Chapel. That was because people didn't go out. They stood around and talked. They told stories on each other. It was country church friendliness at its best. I heard my first, "Reverend Case" and it was like a shock. I hadn't thought of that. 22-years old--*Reverend Case*. Mostly it was Brother Riley, and Sister Ruth. Fred Bushy, with great sincerity, wished us God's richest blessings.

The treasurer asked how much they owed me. That was kind of a surprise too. I didn't realize that was the way things were done. I answered, "The district superintendent said..." She wrote out the check. Nothing like the authority of the district superintendent.

Then came what was perhaps the most memorable part of the day. And this would make it into some future sermons. Rose

Hirschy introduced herself and asked if we would come to her home for dinner. Now Ruth and I may have missed most of the subtle meanings of the morning but, to our credit, we did not miss this one. This was an "official" invitation. Country church protocol demanded the preacher be asked out for dinner. Within five minutes of the closing benediction the country church communication system had been launched with the following results: 1) Rose Hirschy would have the preacher that day, mostly because she was the only one not committed somewhere else; 2) others would donate what food they could. We learned all of this later.

I checked with Ruth. Aunt Selma was expecting us but we would give her a call. This was a fringe benefit I had not anticipated at all: dinner every Sunday. There was some mysterious understanding— unofficial, unorganized, but very effective—as to who would be responsible for the preacher for dinner. In nearly three years at that circuit we did not go without an invitation for Sunday dinner. Seldom did we know where until after the service.

Rose was able to have us because her husband Melvin, was bedfast, and so she usually needed to be at home. Rose became the inspiration for one of my later sermons. The sermon is based on Acts 16:15 and is about Lydia and the gift of hospitality. After Lydia was converted and baptized, "she besought us, saying, if you have judged me to be faithful to the Lord, come to my house and stay, and she prevailed upon us." Hospitality is still around but it is in short supply.

Rose's dinner was typical country dinner for preachers—chicken, mashed potatoes, gravy, and three or four kinds of vegetables. I made my first social blunder in the ministry. I thought her strawberry jam- -it was in a big bowl--was fresh strawberries and I spooned a big heap and ate it with a spoon. Rose served multiple desserts--rural Indiana custom—two kinds of pie, cake, ice cream, cookies. Ruth demurred, but I, wanting not to offend the hostess, ate from all the offerings. Some, I know now, had been sent in by the other women. Rose served them all. Want to impress a preacher? Try serving five desserts.

After dinner we talked, and that talk was worth a seminary course on how to be a minister. It was not a conversation about the weather, nor a conversation between friends; a woman was speaking with her pastor. Ready or not, qualified or not, I was in a new role. Even though she was 40 years older than I, she confided about her life and her son's life and her husband's illness. She spoke about who was sick and who needed a call and who hadn't been in services for a while and who was doing well despite no encouragement from home. She seemed to have full confidence I was going to take care of all the needs of the congregation. I would not wait for the problems to come to me. I would be sensitive to what they were, and handle them before they developed.

Then the conversation shifted to the parsonage and the possibility of seeing it. I was ready to point out that could come later and there were more important things to do. My inexperience showed, not as a pastor, but as a future husband. I should have known that a prospective bride would want to see where we would live. We went to see the parsonage. Rose called ahead to make sure the people at New Corydon knew they had a new pastor and that he would be preaching that evening. They had gotten the word. After seeing the parsonage I do not remember another thing that happened that day.

It was as if the mission were accomplished and everything else was routine. I know there was more to the day from my diary, which always had the uncanny ability to comment on the mundane and miss the essence of things.

Here is the entry,

Nice. (I always had to comment on the weather*) Ruth came in the AM.*

Had my first service at Union Chapel (got lost getting there). Preached on I Cor. 2:2 and had a good time. Ate dinner at Melvin Hirschy's who go there. Saw the parsonage in the afternoon—Ate supper at Aunt Eva's, then to New Corydon for evening service; left from there for Taylor—with Ruth, got Robertson, left for LaGrange. October 14, 1956

The Blood-Washed Banner Of Holiness

"…The blood-washed banner of holiness…" That was just one in a tumbling cascade of phrases in brother Lamoin's gospel message. It was spoken with face flushed and arms upraised and moving, as if the banner were really there, beleaguered, but waving, heralding the unconquerable cause of Christ against the onslaughts of Satan. We were there to do battle, against principalities, against powers, against the rulers of the present darkness. It was all proclaimed in a voice loud enough that all in Hartford Township must surely know, if they did not know already that revival was underway at Union Chapel Methodist Church.

I believed in revivals. I believed in Billy Graham and altar calls and praying through. I knew most of the verses of "Just as I Am." I thought I was revival-trained.

I wasn't. What I knew about were Preaching Missions and Spiritual Emphasis Weeks and Evangelistic Crusades. This was different. This was Revival. This was old-fashioned, Devil-fighting, sin-killing, Methodist Holy Ghost Revival.

The revival was scheduled for fifteen days. That was not fifteen days as opposed to one week, but fifteen days as opposed to six weeks. I was reminded several times that in former days, in the glory days, it took fifteen days just to warm up. But times had changed. The revival would be only fifteen days—unless, of course, the Holy Ghost moved in power. Then the length would be extended as needed.

The district superintendent was uneasy about the revival. "Keep an eye on the revival," he said, "and don't let things get out of hand."

There were innuendos in that statement enough to frighten any twenty-two year old pastor, just three weeks into the ministry. Four weeks before I had been sweeping floors in a factory. I had not the slightest idea how one went about making sure things didn't get out of hand at a revival.

There were other concerns, things that fifty years later I am embarrassed to mention but which seemed big at the time. What was my role? I was the pastor yet this was not really my revival. I had not planned it. I hardly knew my parishioners, let alone the evangelist. Would I introduce him? Would I sit on the platform, or with the congregation? Would I go up and kneel by the pulpit chair to pray, the way I had seen other pastors do, or just go up and sit down? How many offerings would there be? Where would the trumpet trios come from, which were, as far as I knew--having been on a gospel team at Taylor University--indispensable for any revival (how could the Holy Spirit work without trumpet trios)? If souls lined the altar were they my responsibility or the evangelist's? Indeed, who was the evangelist?. All I knew was that it was Brother Lamoin and Sister Gay and they were full of the Holy Ghost.

I spoke with brother O.P. Van Y. O. P. Van Y was my predecessor. Three months earlier O.P. had had a heart attack. The church was without a pastor while they waited for him to recover. Finally the doctor decreed, "No more preaching." That's when I was appointed to the church. O.P.'s visit back to the chapel was his first since the heart attack. He came back because he wanted to be present for the "opening,"—that's what they called it—the "opening" of the revival.

They thronged him that morning at Union Chapel. The country people crowded around O.P. Van Y like ballplayers crowd around a teammate who has just hit the winning home run, or a solider was returned from war, or, probably the way the crowds thronged Jesus when he healed the blind man. They gave him their reports, about the corn yields, about the grandchildren, about ulcers, and who was sick.

O.P. Van Y prayed the closing prayer for Sunday school. It was no simple benediction. It was a one-man prayer meeting. It was a worship service all in itself. After fifty years of preaching, O.P. had been on the sideline for three months. He was making up for lost time. O.P. Van Y beseeched God on behalf of the "chapel," the new pastor, the faithful saints, the coming revival, Brother Lamoin and Sister Gay, souls in the community, the lost, the backslidden, the sick, the weary, the district superintendent, the bishop, missionaries around the world, the Kingdom of God. It there was anyone left out of that prayer I don't know who it was. He didn't just pray. He stormed the gates of heaven and called down angels. He begged and pleaded and cajoled a Mighty God: the Father, the Son, and the Holy Ghost.

The church prayed with him, with groans and amens and hallelujahs, and "Yes, Jesus," and "Oh Lord." I opened my prayer-closed eyes to peek. O.P. Van Y was standing in the aisle. With one hand he gestured Almighty God. With the other, he expertly wielded a white handkerchief, first to wipe a sweaty brow, then a tear-streaked cheek. Through it all he never missed a cadence. I feared for his life. The doctor who prohibited preaching for this man for the sake of his heart should have included public prayers, at least public prayers in country churches on the opening day of revival.

After the prayer the morning sermon, preached by me, was anti-climactic. I don't think the sermon was as long as the prayer. Indeed, the whole service was anti-climactic. I am sure that when people went home and thought of worship on Sunday morning, they thought little about the sermon and a lot about the prayer.

The conversation with O.P. Van Y took place in Forest Shoemaker's living room, where we had both been invited for Sunday dinner following the morning service. There was some problem. The dinner was being delayed. It was delayed for a long time; so we had plenty of time together. Maybe they delayed it on purpose when they heard the conversation.

It was November 4, 1956. What I remember about the day was that the corn and bean fields were clean, all harvested. The leaves were mostly fallen from the trees. It was one of those fall days when sun, sinking lower in the skies, made everything seem brighter. James Whitcomb Riley called it Indian summer.

It was no ordinary day for either of us. With a month of seminary and two weeks into my first appointment, I was full of questions about the ministry, the "Chapel,"—that's what they called Union Chapel—other churches on the circuit, and the revival. Whatever the old circuit rider had to offer I was willing to soak up. I was Elisha waiting for Elijah's mantle.

O.P. had a mantle to give. Ten years ago, they had given him a retirement dinner, but that meant nothing as far as his calling to preach. He would have preached until he died, and very nearly did. He came back that day, nearly fifty years after he had been called to preach and three months after his attack, to make one last stand, to tell his story, to uphold the gospel, and make a witness. I was his only audience.

And so he told his story.

"…I wanted to come back today…the opening of the revival… the doctor said I wasn't ready…doctors don't know everything…good people here, but few young families…I never wanted to quit…doctor said I had to…I suppose he is right…but I had to be here on this day…"

"…we used to have great revivals…six, sometimes eight weeks, morning preaching as well as evening…I was converted in a revival… Muncie…friend wanted me to go…under conviction…Holy Ghost broke through…people prayed at the church all day…1908…God got ahold of me…filled me with the Holy Ghost and called me to preach…it all came at once…"

"I said no…family…twenty-eight years old…no schooling… good job as a glass blower…presiding elder, that is the district superintendent, heard about it, I don't know how he ever knew, I didn't tell him…God must have told him…I hear God called you to preach, he said…I need a preacher in Deerfield next Sunday…I said I couldn't do that but he wouldn't listen, would not take no for an answer…so I was up early next Sunday…twenty miles by horse and buggy…"

O.P. Van Y was sitting on a hassock, hands on knees, not a very tall man, kind of roly-poly, red nose. You remember some things.

"People were friendly enough…I had worked all week preparing…I started preaching and got blessed…I preached for 45 minutes, my very first sermon and then I didn't want to stop…when it was over I realized I had made a terrible mistake…"

The old preacher paused. His timing was impeccable. He could have been in a comedy act. Waiting for the punch line. What was the terrible mistake? O.P. then began to laugh, and he laughed.

"You know what? I had preached everything I had prepared for both morning and evening…everything I knew…I had already preached it and I had another service that night. And I had nothing more to say….Lord, what am I going to do?"

"I was invited to Sunday dinner…so scared I could hardly eat…excused myself saying it was my custom to go to the woods and pray on Sunday afternoon before I had to preach in the evening…I hope the Lord forgave me for a little white lie…well, it wasn't exactly a lie, I was going to start the custom right then and there…headed for the woods…opened the Bible on the stump…prayed…"Lord, help me out of this mess"…wept and read the Bible and prayed and wept and read the Bible and prayed some more….

The old circuit-rider was laughing and crying at the same time…the same big white handkerchief came out of his pocket, he was slapping his thigh and wiping his face.

"We had a great service that night…Lord gave the message…preached another forty-five minutes…anointed by the Spirit…souls converted…people came up afterward and begged me to come back…presiding elder appointed me…I was there three years."

We were quiet then, for a moment, awed by the miracle of long ago. The November shadows were moving across the room. Someone came in and said there were more problems in the kitchen: dinner was delayed even more. For once in my life I was glad. I wasn't ready for dinner just yet.

O.P. wasn't either. He had more stories. From Deerfield we traveled the years across the Indiana countryside through circuits and small towns with stops to dwell on annual conferences, superintendents, bishops, and life in the parsonages. But mostly we dwelt on revivals—ten-weeks revivals, one-week revivals, book burnings, saloon closings, evangelists, families converted. O.P. Van Y's life story and the history of the annual conference was told through revivals.

Then we were back to where we had started, with the revival at the Chapel.

"No need to worry…these people are used to revivals…the church has had a revival a year. They used to have two, as long as anyone could remember."

Then he went through the membership; it was not hard to do with only 40 or so members. He entrusted them all to my care, and laid down the mantle of Elijah.

I went to the church early that night. I intended to greet the people, but I was so new I was the one being greeted. I was introduced to evangelists Lamoin and Gay—she preached when he didn't—to friends and neighbors visiting, and to parishioners I had not yet met. There was a different feeling in the air. The normally joking and easygoing country people had become deadly serious. This was God's hour. Those who waited when the high priest entered the Holy of Holies once a year to make atonement for the sins of the nation would not have been any more impressed by the sanctity of the moment. We were dealing with matters of eternity.

The church was nearly full. The morning attendance, which ran about forty, was doubled. This was revival country. Fringe members who could scarcely make it to church on Christmas and Easter would show up a night or two. Contingents from the other churches on the circuit and from other rural churches near by were there.

The service began. With long involved sentences featuring a syntax wondrous to behold the song leader Glen Dale expressed appreciation for O.P. Van Y, the former pastor, for other friends who were there, for the evangelists, for the good weather, and for the new pastor who had arrived just in time for the revival except he was in seminary and would be leaving after the service to attend school but would be back the coming weekend when he would be a part of the services and everyone was glad for that.

The song service began.

Over the hilltops, down from the skies,
Coming from glory—lift up your eyes!
While we are watching and while we pray,
A mighty revival is sweeping this way.

Sweeping this way, yes, sweeping this way,
A mighty revival is sweeping this way.
Keep on believing; trust and obey.
A mighty revival is sweeping this way.

It was enthusiastic, emotional, and uninhibited. Union Chapel did not know Methodists were becoming more middle-class, tempered, and restrained. There were no businessmen holding half the book and staring blankly with minds set on Saturdays sales, nor elderly ladies who managed to sing by moving their lips only while their teeth were firmly clamped in place. Lorene played the piano country-church style.

Oh, now I see the crimson wave,
The fountain deep and wide;
Jesus, my Lord, mighty to save,
Points to His wounded side.
The cleansing stream, I see, I see!
I plunge and, oh, it cleanseth me!
Oh! Praise the Lord, it cleanseth me!
It cleanseth me, yes, cleanseth me.

Phoebe Palmer, great holiness advocate of 100 years before, wrote that song. It was a great Methodist holiness revival song, but it made few other song books. Plunging beneath a "stream of blood"--modern sensibilities would have none of that. Baptists would not have it; it is a holiness song. It was a favorite at the chapel. It is too bad that song service came so early in my ministry. It would have been a greater encouragement twenty years later when I was sometimes tempted to believe all Methodist congregations had been smitten by the disease of somberness.

Gay and Lamoin sang, pleasantries were expressed, and the sermon began. Revivals featured sermons, or "the message," as it was more correctly called. Everything before—music, offering, singing— was called "preliminaries."

The sermon was about revival. God's people were to get on

their knees and weep and pray. By God's mercy sinners would be converted, backsliders reclaimed, and blessed and sanctified. Besides waving high the blood-washed banner of holiness, we used the shield of faith to quench the fiery darts of the wicked, and lifted a battle cry for the righteousness of God in a sin-sick world.

Thirty minutes or so into the sermon my mind began to wander. Methodists who grew up in county seat towns—like me—weren't used to sermons longer than 25 minutes. I became aware of the people, my parishioners. I who worried that the Methodist Church was too cold and formal—I wondered whether soon I would be under suspicion for being too cold and formal myself. I was pretty sure I would not be waving blood-washed banners of holiness. This little church was beautiful—blond, oak pews, carpet runners—not every church was so equipped. Over on the side, covering a big part of the side wall was a big mural of Jesus with a crook and some sheep. I wondered if the mural was painted free hand. That mural would fit with a sermon already prepared, about Psalm 23 and John 10 and Jesus as the good shepherd. I would preach that sermon soon, I determined.

Finally it was time for the altar call:

All to Jesus I surrender; all to Him I freely give.
I will ever love and trust Him, in His presence daily live.

There was no response to the altar call, but it was only the first night. Christians gathered around the altar to pray for the success of the meeting, and we were dismissed.

I was 240 miles away the next day—back in seminary. Seminary was a different world. We discussed books and movies and spoke in four-syllable words. I still have the class notes. In Pastoral Care and Counseling we talked about learning as the response of the whole organism and how young children do not develop a sense of history and time. In the commons a student told of passing a fundamentalist church where ladies in fur coats carried Bibles. He twirled a cigarette as he spoke. Methodist pastors were committed not to smoke, but he was not yet ordained. The students snickered.

Most of the talk in the seminary was about the election. Tuesday, November 6, 1956. To the seminary community this was a crucial day, the future of America, the world. Would it be Adlai Stevenson and progression, or Dwight Eisenhower and regression? Adlai Stevenson was from Illinois: some of the professors knew him. He was a great man, a thinking man, a sensitive man. Eisenhower was a war man. That night we gathered around the one television set in the lounge to watch the returns.

Gloom. Eisenhower won.

Wednesday was spent analyzing the election and the future of America. In Philosophical Approach to Theology we spent two days hearing about the troubling, disturbing conservative trend in the nation. The election was a sure sign the nation was backing away from social justice and a desire to care for the poor. A dangerous sign was the launching of a new journal, *Christianity Today*. Someone had put free copies of vol. I, no. 1 on a table in the lounge. Was this a resurgence of fundamentalism and right-wing politics?

At Union Chapel they hadn't thought much about Adlai Stevenson, or the future of the country, except as it might be affected by the revival. The report on Friday was that the Holy Ghost had been blessing, but there was no break as yet. They meant there had been no souls at the altar.

The "break" came Sunday night. The church was full—100 or so people. Bill and Margie were there with their three small children. The church had been praying for them. The message was for those who had not been born again, who had neglected God, and would face a tragic judgment if they did not repent. The message was also for those who knew victory, but were backslidden in sin. And then, so that no one would be left out, part of the message was reserved for those wanting sanctification, whose lives were spiritually barren without the fullness of the Holy Ghost.

Just as I am without one plea but that thy blood was shed for me…

On other nights we might sing "Almost Persuaded," or "Pass Me Not, O Gentle Savior." For tonight, the key night, it had to be "Just As I Am." Finally there was movement toward the altar and we sang more verses. Altogether eight persons knelt for salvation, assurance, sanctification, help, or whatever. Bill and Margie were not among the eight. I prayed with Ruby, a high school girl, who wanted to be closer to God. The whole service lasted nearly two and a half hours, but no one complained, at least among the regulars. Prayers were being answered. God had honored the preaching of His word. This could be one of the great revivals.

There had been great revivals at Union Chapel. The unwritten history of the church—the oral tradition—was the story of great revivals. Some churches write their history as the story of buildings, and what preachers came and went. In 1900 the church was built; in 1926 the basement was dug; in 1950 the educational unit was added. In rural America, however, the history of the church is a recounting of the revivals. There was a great revival in 1915, or sometime around there when many had been saved and the meetings were extended for three months. Famous evangelists (whom I had never heard of) preached in the 1920s and 1930s. Many remembered the revival at which they had been converted, or sanctified. They remembered who the evangelist was, where they had been sitting, and who helped them pray through. They remembered when their neighbors had been converted. They made mention of several young men—6 to be exact, who had been called to preach during the revivals.

But it was not to be this time. During the next week I wrote several notes from seminary to let people know I was concerned about the revival. We had no email in those days, we did not use the phone; we wrote. When I got back on Friday I knew this revival was not one that would be remembered in years to come. Bill and Margie had not come back, nor had several others who had been specifically prayed for. The crowd was down to about 40, the usual Sunday morning attendance. The evangelists, Bill and Gay, were preaching to the converted.

The revival closed Sunday night. The crowd was good, the altar call long, but there was no move of the Spirit. No one mentioned extending the revival. O.P. Van Y was back again, and he prayed again, but even that did not bring souls to the altar.

The evangelists were paid $300. That represented 20% of the minister's entire salary for the year. I determined not to share that bit of information with the district superintendent.

In a few days the parish was back to normal. Thanksgiving was coming, and then Christmas. People related to each other with friendly familiarity. There was joking and visiting and talk about winter and corn yields and calves.

There was also an evaluation of the revival. It was not called an evaluation. There were no questionnaires or check lists or committee meetings. There were rather comments dropped here and there: "the lady preacher was every bit as good as her husband…the music was a blessing…there were several fair crowds…good came…" Then a pause. The pause represented the unspoken words, the real evaluation: "…but several people we prayed for were not converted, and we are still needing young couples." There was no church growth from the revival. And without new faces Union Chapel's days were numbered. Numerous little country churches were struggling. More people were driving into town.

It took ten years. I had long since moved. The reports that came were always sad. Attendance was down…a family had moved away… another family started attending church in town where there was more of a youth group.

One day the district superintendent gave the news. The church had voted to disband. They did it in style. They would tear down the building rather than let it stand vacant and deteriorate. Whatever assets were left over they would give to Bashor Home, a home for troubled children. One of the other churches on the circuit could have the pews.

It was some months later when I took the family to see Union Chapel, where "daddy used to preach before they were born." The roads were still graveled. The building was half torn down. The kids were not interested, it was only a building, but I climbed up some boards where I could look into a window. The pews were gone; the piano was gone; the pulpit was gone; but the east wall was standing and the mural of Jesus and the sheep. "He will lead his flock like a shepherd." I did preach that sermon; it was a good one.

Fifty years after the revival, in October, I was at homecoming at Taylor University. An attractive woman approached me and introduced herself. It was Cindy, Cindy Shoemaker, whatever her married name is. She was 55 years old; I know exactly because she was 5 years old when I first went to the chapel. I introduced children's stories there, and she and one or two others were the only ones who sat down in front for the stories. Children's stories were new then; it was a good thing. She remembered. Her father, Glen Dale, the song leader was still living, still serving Jesus, in his 80s. Her grandfather, Forest, one of the most enthusiastic of the revivalists--he waved hankies, an old revival custom, and danced down the aisle—was gone but fondly remembered. I commented that I remembered he still farmed with horses. We agreed life had been good. The people of the chapel that she knew had served well. She was a Taylor grad, I don't remember what she was doing, but she was serving Jesus, and it was good.

And so the church goes on.

"You Cut Down My Tomatoes"

I had just finished preaching my first sermon at Mt. Pleasant. As in the manner of Methodist preachers, at least in the late 1950s, I had not even met the congregation before I showed up on that morning in June. I was mature, at least in my mind. I had almost three years of seminary under my belt and had served one appointment. The Geneva Circuit, with its three churches, was a great place to serve, but it was 250 miles from seminary and the long trip once a week, was wearing, especially now that I was married and we were expecting our first child. Plus, I intended to work on a Master's degree and it would require more trips to Evanston. So I asked for an appointment closer to Evanston, Illinois. Appointments in those days were sometimes like a chess game. Moves were done in strategic sequence and the moves on the student pastor level were the last to be made.

On Thursday of annual conference (10 days before I would preach my first sermon at the new appointment), I saw my superintendent and asked him if they had found a place for me. "Yes, indeed," he replied, "you're going to the Claypool Parish." Good.

But not good. Within 60 seconds of my talk with the superintendent I met a friend, Bob, who was also up for a move. I asked him if they had found a place for him. They had. He told me, "Claypool Parish." So it was in the earlier days of the Methodist itinerancy.

But things were worked out. We moved to Claypool. Three churches: Pleasant Grove, Claypool, and Mt. Pleasant. I didn't get to Mt. Pleasant until the second week. I preached my usual first sermon at a new church, I Cor. 2:2 "I determined to know nothing among you save Jesus Christ and him crucified." I was only 25 years old and I had already preached it six different times, one for each new church up to that point.

Mt. Pleasant was a beautiful country church on a hill. It dated from 1832. It was surrounded on four sides by a cemetery. The country road ran through the cemetery. It was only a mile and a half from Claypool, where we lived, and where there was another of the churches on the circuit. The service at Mt. Pleasant seemed to go well. The people were gracious as they greeted Ruth and me after the service. They were affirming. They always were, at least for the first month of two. After that we were on our own. But today they were smiling. They were introducing themselves and their children and giving a word or two about themselves. "We have three grown children." "We live the next road over." "How do you like your new home?"

Then, all the sudden, someone came by not smiling. Indeed, he had a definite look of unhappiness. "You _____.....tomatoes."

"Excuse me?" I had no idea what he had said. All I got was "You" and "tomatoes."

He said it again. Again I did not understand. So I asked him again to repeat it.

The man behind him came to the rescue. He interpreted, "He told you, 'you cut down my tomatoes.'"

Now I understood what he said, but I had no idea what it meant.

I shrugged my shoulders and greeted more people. I am sure everyone there knew what this was about except me. When there was a break Ralph Reece explained. Ralph was my neighbor in town, a bachelor who cared for his mother. He was the kind of neighbor who checked your lawn to see if it had been mowed. If there was any gossip Ralph knew it.

So Ralph set me straight. The parishioner's name was Luther Lotz. Since the previous pastor knew he was moving he had not planted the garden at the parsonage. Luther got permission to plant it. When I arrived at the new house I found the mower and mowed the lawn. And, in the process I mowed the weed patch at the back. The weed patch was the garden. Under the weeds were the tomatoes. *Were* tomatoes, that is, because now they had been cut down.

So I was not off to a good start with Luther. I needed to patch things up. I was troubled enough about the tomatoes that I asked several people, "Who is this Luther." The answer was something like, "You'll find out."

Well, I slowly pieced the story together. Luther was a bachelor living with two other bachelor brothers down on the south end of town. In one sense they *were* the south end of town; everyone else lived as far north or east or west as they could from the where the Lotz brothers lived. That was because Luther and his brothers had a one-property slum. They single-handedly managed to lower by half the values of any property within shouting distance of them. The property looked a little like a junk yard, though at least officially it wasn't a junk yard. It was just several lots with a lot of junk. I went down several times to make a pastoral call (and to apologize for the tomatoes); I never did get inside the house, or the trailer.

The other two brothers lived in the house. Luther lived in a trailer next to the house. This, evidently, was because the brothers were so angry with Luther for going to church and claiming to be a Christian that they kicked him out. The brothers together had something like 17 dogs, more or less, coming and going, and pigs. This was small town, population 400; they hadn't developed town ordinances about pigs at that time. The pigs lived in town which meant if the wind was in the right direction a big part of the town could smell the pigs, hear the dogs barking and the brothers cursing. The brothers were notorious for their cursing, especially their cursing in loud voices. They evidently cursed the dogs, the pigs, each other, and whatever else, animate or inanimate, was available to curse at.

I asked more questions and received more answers. One man remembered Luther when he was growing up, along with his family, or what there was of it. It was not a pleasant story. It was full of a lot of violence, abuse, cursing, filth, alcoholism, and prostitution. His father was legend in himself; once he carried two railroad ties 5 miles to win a bet for a bottle of whiskey. The children never had much of chance. Several of the children managed to marry and carry on a semblance of a life, but 3 brothers never did; they stayed at home to keep up the tradition. One who made to the 6th grade, or 8th grade, managed to hold down a regular job. Luther had only made it to the 3rd grade; he couldn't get a regular job; he couldn't get a driver's license. However, he managed to buy an old tractor, which he drove around as a means of transportation and which he used in growing some corn and beans and haul hay. He would work for farmers or for whoever would hire him.

It was difficult to think of Luther as a good man, mostly because he was so crude. One of his claims to fame was that he won an egg eating contest by downing 24 fried eggs in a row. I don't know that people necessarily hated Luther. It is just that, well, they were happier when he wasn't around. Luther often gave his opinion, usually with a loud voice, and he didn't care who he offended. He managed to leave enough debts around to make people wary of his presence. Still--the reputation was abroad--that for all his talk Luther was, in the crude vernacular way of speaking, a chicken. He was a coward who would not fight back. Armed with this knowledge the men in town who gathered down at the garage or on the street corners would intentionally antagonize Luther–tease him to get him angry. Grown men can be as cruel as third grade bullies. And Luther, the old Luther, before he became converted, would curse and threaten and then back off and cry. I suppose it went back to the way his father treated him.

But Luther's life had been changed. He told me different times. Sometimes he told me with tears in his eyes. It was because of Frances and Mary, he would say. Frances was a farmer; but he was also a grade school principal. Two boys helped on the farm but they were in high school and busy. The family needed farm help and so they asked Luther if he would work for them. That wasn't unusual. What was unusual was that they invited Luther to live with them in their home. Even that wasn't unusual for hired hands in those days. What was more unusual was that the person they invited was Luther.

It made sense, of course. Luther didn't drive. It was easier for Luther to live with the Reeces than for them to figure how to get Luther to work each day. What the Reeces probably suspected but may not have known for sure was that Luther had never stayed in anyone's home before. He didn't know what it was like to sit at a table for a meal with a family. He told me several times, again with tears, that usually when he went to work for someone they would bring his meal out to him and he would eat in the barn or on the porch. But at the Reeces Luther would sit with the family. Mary would wash his clothes. He could use the living room to watch television.

It was not that they treated Luther in a special way. As he would explain it, they treated him like a man, and they expected him to act like a man in return, and he had never been treated like that before.

Then they asked him to come with them to their Mt. Pleasant church. Luther had tried churches before but, according to him, he was never welcome. At the last church he wanted to sit up in front and the ushers insisted he sit in the back. At Mt. Pleasant, after awhile, Luther attended a revival meeting and was saved.

His life was changed. At least that's what Luther said. That's what the people said. But my thought was, if this is the changed Luther what was his life before? He still chewed tobacco; it would drip down the side of his mouth; he was still loud and opinionated. But, as he would say, he would no longer curse, and that must have been a pretty big victory.

But most of all, he was happy. I don't know how else to put it. He belonged. He did not complain. He was faithful. Always faithful. He was faithful to the Reeces. He was faithful in church. Whenever the door of the church opened Luther was there. Sunday morning, he was there. Sunday school, he was there. Prayer meeting, he was there. Bible study, he was there. Any pot-luck or any time food was served, he was there. He always had his Bible. He bought that Bible after he was converted; it cost him $3. The King James Version. And he insisted on reading it in Sunday school or in the Bible study when we read around the group, even if he had to be helped with the words.

Since Luther didn't drive, and the church was 2 miles out of town, Luther needed transportation. By the time I arrived, it had been worked out. It was usually Blanche. Dear Blanche, she came through town. She was in her forties, had a husband and two teen-agers. It occurred to me later that this was strange, a forty year-old woman picking up a fifty year old man several times a week to bring him to church. But no one thought anything about it. Lots of people in town--I am tempted to say everybody--knew Luther. One winter night it was really bad out, near blizzard conditions. We should have called off Bible study but I never got around to it, so I made it out to the church to see how many people might be there. There were 3 or 4 people so we decided to go ahead with Bible study. About 45 minutes into our study there was a stomp at the door, and Luther walked in; he had walked the 2 miles in the near-blizzard down the tracks. He was mad, "why didn't anybody pick me up?"

Some years later I preached a series of sermons on the beatitudes. The first, Matthew 5:3, is *Blessed are the poor in spirit, for theirs is the kingdom of heaven.* Or, in Luke's gospel, just, *Blessed are the poor.* Jesus probably gave this teaching we call the beatitudes on different occasions, like preachers who give the same, or almost the same message several times. So sometimes Jesus taught, *blessed are the poor,* sometimes blessed *are the poor in spirit.* Either way, I didn't qualify. Furthermore, I didn't personally know very many people who did qualify. If poor in spirit means humble, I knew I was not humble. If poor meant having nothing, I knew that didn't refer to me because I had material blessings without end. In my life I had privilege upon privilege, opportunity after opportunity, health, family, and riches.

Furthermore, it was hard for me to imagine just who among my acquaintances Jesus had in mind. I think in Jesus' generation there were many poor. In our own generation in many places there were poor. But even these poor had resources. And I had a hard time thinking of many people I knew whom I might define as poor as being blessed.

But one person, I believed, qualified. It was Luther and so instead of exegeting the verse like a preacher might, I just told Luther's story.

Here was a man, Luther, with a 3rd grade education. He had no manners, no money, no good qualities that people might like him; and, in the eyes of other men, he was a coward. He couldn't handle what little money he made and few people would loan him any. He was a good worker, but farmers couldn't trust him with their machinery and he was likely to get some job all fouled up. People took advantage of him. If his tractor was in the garage for repair it might or might not get fixed. And when farmers hired him to make hay they would assume he could get along with a sandwich and a glass of milk they would bring out to him on the porch.

There was another way Luther was poor. He was poor in spirit. He had none of what the Bible calls the fruit of the spirit. He was empty spiritually, but with this difference: he knew he was empty. And he wanted something more. That is where he differed from his brothers and from others. Many had nothing inside; but they built up walls to keep everything out. They had a different kind of pride. They fought the world, they cursed their lot; they cursed whatever they blamed for their predicament. They were victims. They blamed whoever put them in their miserable state. They were the ones who live without hope.

I was proud of my little church. Perhaps the story is more about the church than about Luther. I truthfully am not sure Luther could have made it in any other church, at least in other churches I have served. At Mt. Pleasant, Luther had become just one of the believers. Since I had 3 churches to preach at every Sunday I never knew what happened at Sunday School but I would hear about it. Luther talked a lot, whether it made sense or not. He was good for people, although several complained to me more than once they didn't know how much longer they could take it. But they did take it. One man in the class had been a successful doctor in Virginia. He had a beautiful home and family until he got on drugs and lost his practice, his family and his license. He came back home to live with his father and worked in a glove factory while he was getting himself right with God. Eventually he got his license back and became a psychiatrist. Luther helped him. Luther helped a lot of people by keeping them honest. He could spot hypocrisy a mile away. And when he spotted it he told people about it, sometimes to their faces. And they took it.

Churches have personalities. God has a purpose for churches, as he does for families, or for individuals. I have liked all the churches I have served and I do not have favorites. However, one day years later reading through my diary I found several entries where I said that Mt. Pleasant was the most open to the gospel as any church I had served (at least to that point).

The time came when I moved, like Methodist preachers do. So I said goodbye to my parishioners; I was only there three years. A year or so later I read in the *Fort Wayne News Sentinel*, dateline Claypool, that a man had been killed on a tractor hauling hay. It was Luther. I knew nothing about how it happened, nor about the funeral. It was some weeks later before I saw someone from Mt. Pleasant to inquire. Ralph Reece explained… Luther was hauling hay on the highway… truck hit him.

But then I had another question and to me this was far more important. I asked Ralph, "What kind of funeral did Luther have?" His next of kin would have been his brothers. Who knows what they would have planned. I don't know to this day who arranged the funeral but I am sure it was not the brothers. I asked Ralph what to me was a very important question. Did they hold the funeral in the church? Ralph looked rather surprised. It was obviously an unexpected question. He then answered, "Of course."

Then I had another question. "Did anybody come?" I wanted to ask, "Did anybody grieve?" But that would have been too complicated a question. "

Did anybody come?

Ralph said, "Yes…I think the church was full."

The church was full.

"Blessed are the poor in Spirit, for theirs is the kingdom of heaven" (Luke 6:20).

Mt. Pleasant Methodist Church, 1960

Karen Elizabeth Case – 1995

Three By The Stork;
One By United

"Case?" A United stewardess was carrying a bundle—actually a baby--coming off flight 473 from Los Angeles. So this is how it worked? You fill out forms for weeks but in the end someone just comes off a plane and gives it to you? No request for identification. No forms to sign saying we had received the goods. The stewardess handed over the bundle, smiled, and disappeared.

The bundle would be Karen Elizabeth. Of course she didn't know she was Karen Elizabeth. To that point she was Sang Eun Jung, a made-up Korean name really, like Mary Jones. Of course there were a lot of things she didn't know. Such as, she was about to meet her new Mother and Father. She was in a new land. She didn't have to eat ground up cuttlefish any more.

We were at O'Hare Field in Chicago, January 8, 1970. It was 5:00 or so in the afternoon. The plane was supposed to arrive at

12:00. Some kind of delay. The plane had 13 or so Korean orphans coming to the states to be delivered to their new parents. Karen was the youngest. Other children would be 2, or 3, or 7. One girl was 12.

There was a lot of nervousness on the part of all of the parents to be. The trip, all the way from Seoul with a stop in Los Angeles was long enough already. Then to tack on five more hours? I kept having to go to the men's room.

I was telling myself all the time that my reaction was ridiculous. I was nervous about meeting a baby? It wasn't like the president of the United States or something. I didn't have to try to make a good impression. But we were all nervous. Normally I would read to pass the time. But I didn't feel like reading.

It had not been our intention to adopt. We were ready for our fourth child, but it wasn't coming. In the summer of 1968 we visited some friends, Lyle and Nancy Dawson, near Fort Rice, North Dakota, on the Missouri River. It was not a place easily found. Fort Rice is a dot on the map but that does not mean there are people there. The nearest bridge across the Missouri was fifty miles away; church was forty miles away. There on a high bluff at the mouth of the Cannonball River Lyle and Nancy told us the story of their newly-adopted boys. Their story paralleled ours. Wanted more children, weren't getting pregnant, concern about overpopulation, children needing adoption. Ruth wept.

We were ready to explore adoption.

It was before Roe vs. Wade. Five years later the floodgates for abortion would open and babies that would have been available to be placed in homes would never live to have the chance. But in 1968 there was a need for adoptive parents. At least for some children. There was not an oversupply of infants. When we inquired about adoption we were counseled to consider an older child, a special needs child, or to adopt cross-racially or internationally.

Ruth's cousin Maxine and her husband Larry were in the same situation. Three boys-- they wanted a girl. They spoke of Holt Adoption Agency. It was further confirmation. Holt Adoption Agency grew out of the compassion of one couple from Oregon. After the Korean War, when U.S. servicemen had fathered way too many children in a far-off land, stories were circulating about abandoned babies stigmatized by an unaccepting culture. World Vision was one of the Christian agencies that moved in to try to care for the babies. One night at a church in Oregon an appeal was made for funds to help World Vision care for the orphans. One couple, Harry and Bertha Holt, felt that money alone was not enough. Their farmhouse was big. Perhaps God had given them a big house for a purpose. They could take some of those children. There was no provision for this, but Harry Holt, an uncomplicated man, did what he felt was a very logical thing. He got on a plane to Korea with the intention of bringing back orphans.

The story got messy at that point. People don't just pick up and bring back orphans from foreign countries. But Harry Holt was not easily defeated. He stayed in Korea. A friend of ours says he saw Harry Holt in that period. He was a middle-aged man on his own in a run-down hospital trying by himself to care for 25 crying babies.

Harry Holt's story hit the newspapers. It took an act of Congress but Harry Holt brought back eight orphans. By now the story was out and the Holts, with help, set up what would become Holt Adoption Agency.

Holt seemed an answer to prayer for the child we wanted. By the late 1960s the U.S. soldiers were no longer in Korea, but Korea was still recovering from the ravages of war and there were children needing homes. In some instances Mothers gave up their babies with the belief the babies would have a better life in America. The application was time-consuming. Actually, it was not the application for adoption that was complicated; it was working with Immigration and local welfare agencies. The process took several months.

Finally we were approved. The day came when we received word of a child for us, a baby who had been abandoned. With the notification came a picture. For months we stared at the picture—our only link with this child--and prayed. We wondered where she was and who was caring for her. The answer was she was at the orphanage; then she was in a foster home. Finally the word came: send clothes and then go to O'Hare on January 8, 1970.

Then the questions. Would we bond? This was really not an

infant but an eight-month old child. How would she be affected by whatever had happened during the eight months? Was it the same for an adopted child as with a birth child?

It did not matter. Nothing mattered when the stewardess handed over the child. A strange something-or-other happened. It was the overwhelming presence of God. It was grace. Maybe irresistible grace. I believe I never was so close to being a Calvinist as at that moment. It was like, "You have been chosen." Something different even from the three times we had for the first-time held our new-born baby. The others came, well, expectedly. We had been a part of the creation. Moving, but in a different way. This time it was like God had said, "I have chosen you for this child, and this child for you." Three came by the stork; one by United Airlines.

We wept. We were not alone. Thirteen Korean children got off the plane. Thirteen sets of parents, along with other family members who had gathered at O'Hare, from surrounding states: Iowa, Minnesota, Michigan—all were weeping. A stranger coming on the scene would have been mystified. The Korean children, many toddlers, some older, were not weeping. They were looking bewildered.

Our baby was scared. She did not respond to the hug and the kiss. She pulled away. Her look was something like panic. Her breath smelled. I assumed it was because of Korean food we knew nothing of. I also guessed it was ground up cuttlefish. No mind. We knew this would change.

We met the missionary assigned to accompany the Korean children, a missionary whose plane fare to the states was paid by Holt in exchange for accompanying the children. He had parented all thirteen children for the hours in the air. But now it was our turn.

We had not been worried about the trip home, to Elkhart. We should have been. All afternoon the sun had been shining. It was cold, near zero, but it was sunny. But as we drove toward Indiana the sun disappeared and we hit snow. Lots of snow. Heavy, drifting snow. It was lake-effect snow. But that made it no less threatening. The sun could shine at O'Hare but twenty miles around Lake Michigan there was a blizzard. By now it was dark and getting hard to see.

January, 1970. Case children: Jeremy, Jay, Karen, Cris

Near Michigan City we blundered. We missed the exit onto the Indiana toll road from I-80 and we were in Michigan. We would have to take an alternate route, U.S. 12, in Michigan, to Niles. By this time there were blizzard conditions. We had our Chevy II, a plain-Jane car. No radio. We couldn't hear how far the snow extended east.

Our baby was asleep. Who knew what time she was on? This was in the days before mandatory car seats. Her cradle was Ruth's arms. We were thankful she was not awake.

Suddenly I became frightened. I don't think I ever worried about bad roads before. But I had never been responsible for an eight-month old baby before in a blizzard. We had not prepared well. We had to find milk at O'Hare. I couldn't see the side of the road. I couldn't see much of anything; the snow was coming so hard. We could not stop, lest we be rammed from behind. At the same time, we had to drive slowly lest we hit a car stopped in front. There were no landmarks. Nothing looked familiar.

I prayed as I had not ever prayed before. "Lord, help us get home." It was more complicated really. "Lord, you have chosen us to be parents of this child. Lord, help us to be good parents. Give us love for her (as if that was needed—we had already been overwhelmed by love). Lord, we know you have great plans for her but first we have to get home. We have to get to a town at least." I tried to calculate the miles but there were no mile markers.

Even though it was only 7:00 at night, we met almost no cars; saw no lights. It was like we were on country roads in North Dakota. If we were stuck in a snowbank I had no idea where to walk. We had maybe a bottle of milk, but what after that? If stranded how long would it take for the idled car to run out of gas? How long before a car without a heater drops to freezing?

I can't remember everything I prayed but I think my mind was wondering off into my purpose in life, my calling as a minister. "Lord, I believe you have things for me to do but first I have to get home."

Well, we made it. We came into Niles and then came south to South Bend. At that point we were on familiar territory. As for our baby, she was marvelous (through no effort of ours). Later we would have long nights of crying. She would wake up screaming as if having nightmares. It took several days before she could smile. She would be stiff, but eventually she would relax.

We remember those tough days. There were long nights singing, "Amazing Grace," alternated with "Rock-a-By Baby," with maybe a Wesley hymn thrown in, something like "And Can It Be That I Should Gain an Interest in the Savior's Blood?" If the child was going to grow up remembering songs sung, the songs might as well be something edifying.

We arrived home in Elkhart at 8:15. We had not checked out watches but it was half-way through the The Brady Bunch and they came on at 8:00. There was a contest in the TV program between the boys and girls as to how could build the biggest stack of cards. Ten years later on the re-runs our kids found out how the show came out (the dog Tiger knocked down all the cards). Whenever they would see the rerun again they would call out the exact spot in the show when their new sister came through the door.

My parents were there. No one there had any sense that we had just about died in the Great Blizzard of 1970. Of course it was surely, looking back years later, not as serious as it seemed.

The Lord knows those things. He probably allows us to think

these things so we would trust him more.

In 1991 we went back to Korea—Ruth, Karen, and I. We always told Karen we would go back sometime after high school. We visited the Holt orphanage. The only new information we gathered was that she had been found in a port city in southern Korea, not in Seoul as we had imagined.

In Korea, Karen did not stand out, at least as far as Ruth and I were concerned. In the states we could always pick her out in a crowd. She was the Korean child. In Korea she was just like everyone else. She was even the same size. Except she wasn't just like everyone else to the Koreans. She drew stares. It was her hair style and her clothes. Young guys tried to talk to her, but of course she understood nothing. She was thoroughly American.

She did not like the food. We always told her the Lord sent us to deliver her from cuttlefish.

The Killdeers Are Back

"The killdeers are back." I paused from the book I was reading. The words had come from "Grandpa" Unkenholz (Ruth's father) as he stuck his head in the kitchen to announce he was in for lunch. The words were spoken to no one in particular, I believe. Not necessarily to me, I am sure. I was in the laundry room, several rooms away. The laundry room was my favorite place under the circumstances, the circumstances being that that was the only quiet place to read.

"The killdeers are back." Maybe it was the tone of voice. It was like an affirmation. It was not that I had any interest in killdeers (I was still 12 years away from what would become a bird-watching passion). That killdeers should come back to North Dakota in the spring was not significant information. Who cared? Well, I guess I cared. The words could have been spoken a thousand other times and they would have held no special significance. But at that particular moment they had significance. It was not just that killdeers were back. It was rather that spring was coming, God was in control, and all was well in the world.

It was vacation time, late March, 1970. Not a normal time for vacation, to be sure. At least not in North Dakota. It was Ruth's idea. Every summer we had made the annual pilgrimage to the farm, a pilgrimage I had not counted on when we first were married. The farm was a great place, home for Ruth to be sure, but I had not been thinking ahead. It had not occurred to me that summer vacation time would be committed to the farm for the next forty years.

Ruth had been thinking ahead. Five days into our honeymoon in the Black Hills some years before, Ruth announced suddenly we needed to get back to the farm. Evidently everyone gathered at the farm on the 4th of July. Everyone meaning family, neighbors, church people, friends. Of course in rural North Dakota even with all those people there was not too big a crowd. It was then I realized that getting back to the farm was the expectation not only for July 3, 1957, but for once-a-year vacations for years to come.

It's a good thing we went back. I had a grand total of 13 cents in my pocket when we pulled into the barnyard late on July 3. This was in the days before we had credit cards and we had seen only a car or two the last 50 miles of our trip.

So we made our annual trips to the farm. During the year we would see my parents many times. Once a year we would see her parents for a week or two in the summer.

Except in 1970. We had missed the farm in 1969, for reasons which escape me now, and would miss again the summer of 1970. My parents had asked us to spend a week in Wisconsin. So Easter break, 1970, was the compromise. We would take two vacations that year and this one would be to the farm.

I foresaw problems. I was getting used to the farm; indeed, I was beginning to look forward to our vacations on the farm. But in April? Doesn't it blizzard in North Dakota even in April? There could be no golfing. For the past 13 years golfing had kept me occupied. But there would be no golfing in April. Snow was still on the ground. And the children, four children 10 and under, including Karen, newly arrived, less than 3 months from Korea. Eleven months old, she was still waking up in the middle of the night, screaming. There would be more of that at the farm. And so the prospect: cooped up in the house for two weeks with all those children with no golfing.

Packing had been a nightmare—boots and coats and flannel shirts and spring outfits and matchbox cars and dolls and diapers and crackers—trying to organize this and pack it all into a small Chevy II station wagon with a big luggage carrier. And this at the busiest time in the calendar, Good Friday and Easter. But we made it. 1:40 Easter afternoon, we were off.

I was depressed. I didn't know it at the time. Later, I realized: I was depressed. Our attendance for Easter was 453. Last year we had had 534. Preachers get bothered by such things. Angels may not care as much. I rationalized. Last year we had a choir cantata and two services. This year the school break came the week after Easter. Folks were gone.

The people in the service seemed restless. Easter services never go quite right. Regulars were frustrated because some of the once-a-year attenders got there and were sitting in their pews. There were some different faces but not as many as I would have liked. The new people were cautious, uneasy, not really at home in church. Singing was not that great; the once-a-year crowd never sings well. The regulars weren't as friendly as they should have been. Not quite the Easter exuberance we always hoped for. In the sermon I scolded people for wanting Easter joy without Good Friday suffering and spoke of the three-hour Good Friday services we used to have at Ashley, where we served before Elkhart.

Bad move, to compare the church you are pastoring with the one you had pastored before. I was unhappy with myself for letting it slip out.

There were other reasons for depression, bigger reasons. The world was blowing apart. A week or two earlier I had a conversation with a bridesmaid at a wedding rehearsal dinner. She was angry, maybe because she had to sit next to the preacher. I suspect, however, she was angry because she was a child of the times. Part way through her T-bone steak at the Holiday Inn she started her harangue, against the war, against the government, against the church, against Richard Nixon, against history classes. I understood all the rest but why take it out on history? "What's wrong with history?" I asked meekly.

"It has nothing to say to me." It was not that I had not heard this before. It was just that I had not expected it at a rehearsal dinner at the Holiday Inn at what was supposed to be a happy occasion with some of my church members. Even college students at rehearsal dinners ought to make some attempt to be civil.

But times were bad. Two years before, April, 1968, Bobby Kennedy had ridden by our house in an open convertible. He took the route he did in order to ride through the black community. We waved. A few days later he was killed. Shortly before that Martin Luther King had been killed.

Race riots broke out, not only in Watts, and in Detroit, where cities burned, but also in our town—Elkhart, Indiana. People threw rocks and marched and screamed. There were police lines and police dogs. It was a good time to stay at home and wait it out.

Jeremy, Jay, and Riley, North Dakota,
April 1, 1970

It wasn't to be. One night a crowd marched on city hall. They made demands. The spokesperson was Simon Peter Montgomery. I groaned. Simon Peter Montgomery was in my church, Calvary Church. He was a United Methodist minister brought to town to head the Urban League, attracted to the church by my predecessor, Dwight Conrad. They had both gone to Boston Seminary, where, everyone knew, Martin Luther King had also gone. Simon Peter Montgomery never ceased to talk about Martin Luther King, like a close friend; I suspect he was more like an acquaintance, but never mind. Simon Peter Montgomery was going to lead the charge. Simon Peter Montgomery was not necessarily a close friend; he called me up in the middle of the night once to come to his house where he and some of his other friends dumped on me. He was seldom in church. His wife and kids were always there; I don't know where he went. But he was still my parishioner, under my pastoral care.

The day after the march on the mayor's office a White Citizens Council was formed. Three hundred angry whites had their own rally. They spoke of confrontation. It was scary. There were big banner headlines in the paper.

Then I got a call. It was a preacher friend, Joe Wagner. "Do you know who the leader of the White Citizen's Group is?"

"No."

"Jim Sanders." I groaned. That would be my parishioner, Jim Sanders. He was also angry. The town was divided between angry blacks and angry whites and the leaders of both groups were from my church.

"You have to do something," Joe said. It was like a demand.

Well, what we did is another story. A long story. It involved the labor unions, calls in the middle of the night, the mayor's office, and a new friend, Bob Dungy, a hero of sorts in the whole thing, who at that very time had a young nephew named Tony. Bob later also became a UM pastor. Tony became a football coach but that was years later also.

At the moment we were sitting on a powder keg. On top of this the church was in turmoil. The charismatic movement had hit; Elkhart seemed a center. People were divided for and against speaking in tongues. Then the Jesus People showed up, and one of the most aggressive of them all was Doug, one of my lapsed members who in his testimony spoke of fighthing with Satan and came to tell his story in my church, to the delight of our youth and to the horror of the parents. Another long story.

Our church was involved with some of the churches in a coffee house ministry in downtown Elkhart. Town leaders said it was a center for drugs. Another story.

More problems. A motorcycle gang visited our church. Another long story. People who say that the 1960s were marvelous times didn't live in them. At least in Elkhart, IN, and especially in the kind of church I was serving. Later I would come to believe those were the most exciting months of my ministry. But at the time I didn't think so.

So we left town. Maybe an April vacation wasn't so bad after all. Eighty miles out of Elkhart I was feeling a bit better already.

"The killdeers are back." That part came about halfway through the vacation. There were other concerns related to the farm. Just months before Ruth's brother Jim, who, it was assumed would take over the farm and keep it in the family, had given up. Drought, bad prices, no money. Jim had a college degree in agriculture; he had big plans, but it wasn't going to work. There was no future in the farm without major investment and there was no money for major investment. So Jim and his wife Lee and their three kids had moved to Evanston, IL, where Jim enrolled at Northwestern to pursue education credentials.

Ruth's father was 75 years old. What was to become of him and of the farm? Ruth and her sister and brothers grew up on the farm. Before that her father grew up on that farm. Before that his father homesteaded the land and grew up there. Was it now to be in the family no more? And why did I, who had only married into the family, care so much?

We also discussed the school. Rural school. The one-room school. Ruth's school. The Unkenholz school. The school had been there for 90 years. But there were only 8 or 10 students in the school. Times were changing. Next year the 7th and 8th graders would go to town. A school bus route was being scheduled. It would be an hour on the bus, too long for little kids, plus many days the busses would not get through. But it was only a matter of time. The Great Plains were in the midst of change, and there was nothing we could do about it. At the moment the school teacher lived in the second house on the farm. When he left there be no other people living within a mile.

And the church? Small enough as it was, with Ruth's brother and family gone, it was smaller still. How long could it hold on? Propsects for the future? Not good.

"The killdeers are back." If there was stress, or pressure, or worry, it had not seemed to affect Grandpa Unkenholz. He noticed a crocus in the pasture. He was excited about a little cedar tree that had seeded itself and was about to launch a new life in the shelter belt. Every time he came into the house he discovered something new. Spring.

It didn't look much like spring to me. I saw no green. The drifted snow in the shelter belt was still eight feet deep. But Ruth's father saw the signs. The buds on the trees were swelling. Ducks were flying overhead. He showed us some buffalo horns he had found and polished. Ruth asked me what ever happened to the buffalo horn she had given to me when we were dating. I guess at the time I was not greatly impressed. The buffalo horn was gone, someplace or other. Suddenly I wished I had it back. That buffalo horn, found in the pasture, seemed a treasure.

The weather was beautiful. It was unseasonably warm. One day it was 80 degrees. It was warmer in Bismarck, North Dakota, than in Florida. Jay and Jeremy and I walked on top of the drifts in the shelter belt. We took our shirts off and played in the snow. We walked down to the coulees, the little ridges and valleys where snow collected. One day we went farther. Jeremy (age 5) got snow in his boot, and wanted to go back. Jay and I went on. The snow was melting, little streams were running here and there. We played. I reminded him that when I was his age I built dams when the snow melted. We built dams, and tried to redirect the water. It was good.

On April Fool's Day we did our tricks, Ruth and I. We changed the cereal in the boxes so that when the kids thought they were pouring Cheerios they were getting Rice Krispies; we put Pepsi-cola in the milk pitcher so they poured pepsi on their cereal. We turned the clocks 2 hours ahead and told the kids it was time for bed so that when the clock said 9:00 and it was really 7:00. They objected but they were obedient. After they were in bed a while we went into their rooms and said "April Fool." We got them up and had snacks and let them stay up late. It was great fun. Every night I told them my outrageous children's stories. It was good.

Every morning in that house, as had been the custom for the last 75 years, ever since the land was homesteaded, Ruth's father, and his father before him, and his father before him, got down the family Bible and we heard the word, and had our prayer. No one left the table until prayers were said. And it was good.

And then for what seemed like for hours I walked our little Korean orphan and held her tight because she was still a troubled little girl. Our vacation had not been a good idea as far as she was concerned. She was only getting used to Elkhart; now we brought her to a strange place and more strange people. There was a lot of walking. And singing. "Jesus Loves Me" and "Rock-a-by-Baby" and

"Victory in Jesus." At the time I prayed for her to relax and go to sleep. Years later I remember it with fondness. You walk with a person for an hour and sing songs. You bond. It was good.

Toward the end of the stay we fought a prairie fire. Clouds of smoke in the distance. Ruth's brother Dick was there. We thought we would do our duty. We assumed all the neighbors would come to the rescue, maybe the town fire department, and fight the prairie fire. I had read about those things. Fires out of control, burning houses, killing livestock.

Actually it wasn't nearly that dramatic. This was a short-grass prairie fire with little tiny flames, and it wouldn't burn in the coulees where the snow was. Furthermore, no one else seemed all that concerned. But we were, Ruth's brother Dick, and I, and Jay. We would save the world, save the farmsteads, save the homes. Fighting that prairie fire was like fighting evil. We put snow in gunny sacks and beat the ground. The front of the fire was one mile, maybe two miles wide. After a while we gave up. The farmsteads, what few there were, would be on their own. We learned later that the fire may have been started deliberately, to burn the prairie grass off.

When I was not with the kids, not playing in the snow, not drinking coffee at the kitchen table, not fighting prairie fires, I read, in my little hide-out in the laundry room, 6 or 8 books; serious books, Jacque Ellul, Francis Schaeffer and a book on Greek and Hebrew Thought Compared. The books made good sense. Marvelous minds, bringing order in a disorderly world. Too much to do, back in Elkhart, to do serious reading. On this vacation, especially with no golf, there was time.

Finally our stay was up. It was hard to say goodby. We were leaving Mother and Father Unkenholz, 75 years old, alone on the whole farm. Well, not exactly alone. The killdeers were back. The crocuses were blooming in the pasture. The little spruce that reseeded itself, was growing. The North Dakota friends, even if none were closer than a mile, were there.

We put back all the stuff in the little Chevy II station wagon with the luggage carrier, boots and coats and spring outfits and books and matchbox cars, and diapers and crackers, and six of us and started our thousand mile journey. We drove around where the prairie fire was. It was still burning. Maybe it wasn't such a big thing after all.

On the way home we sang and played games and had our surprises and ate at McDonalds; hamburgers were 23 cents. The kids always remembered the trips. We were glad to be home.

I was thankful. I had been restored. We were by no means through the worst of the times. In a few short weeks Kent State would happen, May, 1970. We weren't through the worst of the riots and the demonstrations and angry bridesmaids and turmoil in the church but I must say, they didn't seem nearly as threatening.

For I had heard the killdeer, and seen the spring crocuses in the pasture, and the little cedar trees in the shelter belt and experienced the prairie fire and the morning prayers, and felt the quiet confidence of Father Unkenholz. I had built dams in the coulees with my son, and sung at night to my daughter, and told ridiculous stories at bedtime.

And I was reminded of a promise in the Bible, made back when times were really troubled, after the world had been destroyed, not by a prairie fire nor by riots but by a flood, after Noah came off the ark and made an altar. At that time God smelled the smoke, and said in his heart:

While the earth remains, seedtime and harvest, cold and heat, summer and winter, day and night, shall not cease (Gen. 8:22).

Brown Spots And Blue Birds

Edna Mae Burkhalter Case, 1900-1982

Brown spots. My mother's brown spots; like constellations in the sky, only these were freckles and birthmarks on her left arm in their own distinctive pattern. As unique as a person's voice, or a fingerprint.

How were they impressed on my memory? Perhaps when…

…*I was on her lap, maybe age 2. I was laughing, pushing her breasts. She was holding my hands, moving them away…*

…*We were at the piano; I was in high school and our quartet was practicing; I was watching her play…*

…*I had my fingers around her wrist, comparing her thicker wrists with Ruth's thinner wrists….*

And now, I was holding her same hand in the hospital room, and suddenly I recognized the pattern of her brown spots.

I wept.

Mother was dying. The bone cancer had eaten her away so that her body was like a hollow shell. The patterned brown spots seemed the only identifiable part of her.

Our family was not handling the death particularly well. There was no gathering of all the children and grandchildren to say farewell. No hymn singing. No final memorable words like preachers talk about when Christians die.

It should not have been surprising. It fit her personality. She often dealt with pain by avoiding it. For months she did not want to admit she was terminally ill. She did not want to speak of dying, or even of heaven. She did not make desperate appeals to be on prayer chains. We did not know of hospice then. Even had we known about it, I suspect Mother would not have wanted it.

One could call it denial. I realize I am a lot like that. I had always assumed I got that from my father but it was probably my mother. It made her dying more difficult.

There was a lot of love in our family but we did not express it well. We did not hug a whole lot, especially on Mother's side of the family. No touching or kissing among the relatives; they were not given to that. Father's side hugged some, at least the women did. Sometime early in life I realized I needed to stay away from my (great) Aunt Nellie and my father's cousin Mary Holsinger. They hugged, and they had the kind of bosoms in which a little kid could smother to death.

Mother once remarked, after a time of living around the Cases, that it did not seem right that she was to hug my father's family while she never hugged her own family. If she tried to introduce hugging among the Burkhalters she failed miserably.

Mother was from Berne (Indiana). It was a cloistered community, centering around the largest Mennonite Church in the world. Mennonites are cautious with their emotions. In those days they did not yell or scream or hug. Still, the ties of family, church, and community were strong, as well as suspicion of the outside world. In the 1940s when I would spend five weeks there each summer attending Bible school, I was aware of the "us" and "them" mentality. Outsiders were suspect. I remember my Aunt Selma, Mother's twin sister, talk about the "Yankees." I wasn't sure who Yankees were but I knew they were not our kind. Later in life I figured it was probably Methodists who lived in Geneva (5 miles south).

Mother's grandmother, Mary Lugibhil, may have been the most Mennonite of all. Mother spoke of her a lot. In 1874 Mary Lugibhil came from Putnam County, Ohio, another Mennonite community, to Adams County, Indiana, to stay with relatives and (it is presumed) to find a husband. One day she encountered Peter Burkhalter at the clothes line. Peter, a neighbor, for some reason was bringing by a pig. Peter and Mary talked. On Saturday he came back. They took a walk. Wondering if the Lord had a message for them, they opened up the Bible. The finger fell on Psalm 45, the royal wedding Psalm ("Instead of your fathers will be your sons…"). They concluded that God had willed for them to be married. They had eleven children, four of whom became missionaries. One of the seven who did not become a missionary was my grandfather Amos.

Riley L. Case and Edna Burkhalter - 1926

The Burkhalters lived in obedience to God. And for family. According to Mother her grandmother, Mary Lugibihl Burkhalter, prayed by name each night for the salvation of every one of her children, and her grandchildren, and those to follow to the third and fourth generation, whose names she did not know. When this story is related today my children tell their children they have to start on their own because the blessings prayed down by their great-great-great grandmother have run out.

The blessings had not run out for Mother. She believed she was covered by those prayers. That was the key to Mother's life—prayers, blessings, family. The grandmother's prayers were only part of it. There were also the prayers of parents, sisters, aunts, uncles, great-aunts, cousins--Mennonites all, for generations. They were 100% pure Mennonite blood for as far back as anyone had been able to keep records. Back to the high mountains of Switzerland and beyond.

One does not break the bonds of those family ties easily.

Shipshewana, though, was a test. Mother had gone to a

Mennonite College, Bluffton, and had taught school near Berne. Then she tried out the world. When she was 25 and single she moved Shipshewana, Indiana, to try life away from Berne. Shipshewana was one of the Mennonite centers of the world, but inexplicably, Mother ended up in the Methodist Church.

Perhaps not inexplicably. The Mennonites of Shipshewana--and there were many--were the wrong kind. One must be knowledgeable about the nuances of conservative Christianity to understand. Shipshewana Mennonites were the kind that wore prayer caps. Mother did not do caps. Better to be a Methodist than a Mennonite wearing caps.

Furthermore, the Methodist church was where my father was, sort of, as well as all of the important people of the town, to the extent that a town of 300 can have important people. At least the teachers were there, including the young adult set. Mother probably would not have wanted to be so accused, but she was being tempted by the "world," or at least the Shipshewana social scene.

My father, the principal of the school, had hired her as the music teacher. He took criticism from the community because he brought in an outsider. My guess is that he thought a young, single attractive 25-year old music teacher was just what the school (and perhaps he) needed. At any rate, not long into the school term when Mother was in charge of the school assembly, my father, known as the stern principal, walked into the assembly room, looked around as if something were the matter (my mother's words), and approached her desk. She was thinking reprimand for something or other. Instead he leaned down, and in a whisper, asked her for a date.

That was typical Riley L. Case. He didn't do romance well. Novelists write books about torrid love stories. From the letters I read and from my mother's journal my parents' courtship would hardly qualify as torrid. At the same time it was certainly not without drama.

Their courtship, if that's what it could be called, lasted six years. My sister Ann dated Tom, her husband, for eight years, but they had started in the eighth grade. My father and mother were different. They started when my father was 29. My mother had reached 25, already well along in life for a young Mennonite woman needing to start home and family. Father was handsome and successful and highly regarded and eligible. But he was not from Berne. The Berne relatives were appalled (I have reason to believe) that my mother would consider a Methodist, and from all indications, an unsaved Methodist at that. The Case relatives were supportive, though I sense they thought Mother far too religious.

As the years dragged on my Aunt Gay, my father's sister, said she despaired that anything would ever come of the relationship. Her brother had already given up the Masonic Lodge for Edna but she wanted more. She wanted him to join her church (for Aunt Gay that was the Methodist church in Shipshewana). The Cases had been Masons ever since the Revolutionary War. I doubt if my father thought he was giving up much, since I never heard him talk about the Masons, but Aunt Gay saw this as a sacrifice on Father's behalf to make the relationship work.

The Shipshewana people waited patiently. I'm not sure it was too public a romance, it being, after all, the principal dating one of the teachers, but everyone knew. The single females, most of whom were my mother's friends (as well as rivals), were waiting in the wings in case the courtship faltered. The Methodists, I am sure, were pulling for marriage. Mother had become active in the church. Father not so much. Mother was urging him to join. As a couple they would make a nice addition to the church.

Meanwhile, whether single or coupled, Mother was active in Shipshewana's young adult social scene, if her diary can be believed. She had a circle of friends; she went to ball games and school activities; she was frequently at someone's house for a meal; she was active in church; she attended concerts; she went often to LaGrange, Goshen, and Elkhart, the nearby larger towns. She played cards and reported the gossip of the town.

She also showed spunk. Her diary from Feb. 6, 1928:

Some rowe with Monty about Sunday nite... Welti was in the office. Nona contradicts the girls' story at first but has to give in. ...Steve rove about the day. Decide to hold my own after arguing with Monty and holding up dismissal for 10 minutes. He said to sleep over it. Crazy.

(Next day)

Ready to argue again. Expect to win. Talk and argue for 20 minutes about Latin contest. Monty is simple in his arguments. He finally gives in. "Against his will" he says at noon. I call LaGrange. Caton Bros. Monty walks in. We find out a few nasty things he said to his. students. He talks to her but I must not tell. Expect a chance but only Mrs. Morgan follows.

(Next day)

Mr. Monty is certainly anything but pleasant.

My father was at Indiana University while Mother is asserting herself at Shipshewana. He was working on a Master's Degree. She reports on the highs and lows of letters and contacts with him.

January 1, 1928

What of 1928? Hope it to be a better one than the year before…

August 30, 1928:

Lovely moonlight night! But it doesn't do me any good. Case cold, colder, and coldest. Where's my kiss? My reward?

August 26, 1928

Yann met me in Kendallville. Go to his folk's place. Play the piano. Very nice. But I do not allow kiss on my lips. Wonder if I should have. Well he doesn't deserve it.

"Yann" was the name used by those who knew Father growing up. When he went to Shipshewana he became "Case." Mother didn't like either of those and, after they were married, got everyone to call him "Riley."

It was probably best I was not reading the diary when I was in junior high. I believe I would have been upset if I thought my parents ever had problems. Father never spoke of such things. In his version it was probably boy meets girl; they get married, and live happily ever after.

But for Mother it was a long, and often frustrating, ordeal. She talked about it once. Only once that I remember. I'm not sure who else she ever talked with, other than her sisters, and perhaps my sisters, later. The story was told me in the car on the way to my first day at Taylor University. Father was not along, and that, I believe, was part of what triggered the story. Mother was disappointed. First child in college…a tender moment…both Fathers and Mothers need to be there. Actually it did not matter to me at all if Father was not present. I didn't think I needed parents for such things. I had more of my father's genes in regard to these things.

(And evidently, so did my sister Ann, who did not want either parent with her when she showed up for her first day of school in the first grade. She was, after all, a big girl now. She walked into the school building alone and found out she was the only first grader without a Mother.)

According to the account in the car, my mother and father almost did not get married. Mother explained: religion. His upbringing was far different from hers. She wanted a Christian family. Father was far too nonchalant about such things. He dragged his feet about joining the church. She did not speak of his perspective but I suppose he had far too much integrity to be forced into something he was not ready for. Finally he relented. He made a public confession and joined the church.

With that taken care of, after six years, the wedding came quickly. On December 26, 1931, over Christmas break, they were married. Aunt Gay, Father's sister, said she knew about the wedding only the day before and had not brought an appropriate dress. Father and Mother may have been the only people in the world to spend the first night of their honeymoon in Huntington, Indiana.

Back in Shipshewana, friends already in place, Mother and Father launched into their many years of social life. There were continual rounds of outings and activities. There were Shipshewana friends, and after they moved to LaGrange, LaGrange friends. There were relatives on her side and relatives on his side. There were also Purdue friends, especially my father's Agathan (fraternity) house. There were church friends and neighborhood friends and county agent friends. My sisters and I grew up with a steady stream of baby-sitters. Later there were Rotary friends.

Mother and Father were opposites in many ways. She was the extravert (she hated to be alone) and he the introvert. She was right-brain: music and art and decorating. He was left-brain, detailed, meticulous and careful. He could have devised the Franklin Planner system.

He was cautious in driving; she was an adventuresome driver. She complained about trucks driving slowly and, instead of urging her husband to slow down like most of the wives of the world, urged him to speed up. ("Pass him!") Perhaps the most exciting of her driving adventures was getting the letters to the 4:15 train going south. Letters delivered by 4:15 to the box at the station would arrive in Berne the next day. She piled the family into the car and drove like we were in a car chase in the movies. When we could hear the train whistle we broke many, many town ordinances. We would slam to a stop and I would run to catch the conductor who was ready to board the train with mailbag in hand.

Father liked to be on time. Mother was fashionably late. He went to bed early. She went to bed late. He liked to save. She liked to spend. He recorded the money spent to the last penny. His plan for keeping track of the groceries was to replenish a "grocery purse," from which all groceries were to be purchased, with $20 and $40 or whatever. Mother learned to keep receipts but when she forgot and was forced to sit down and try to remember what had been purchased and what it cost it sometimes elicited my father's favorite expletive, "Ach." After she died we found envelopes with money or checks in them for honorariums for bird talks she had given which she had thrown in the drawer and forgotten. My father was appalled.

This is not to suggest she was sloppy. She, after all, had grown up Mennonite and in Berne. In Berne there was social pressure to keep houses clean and clothes clean and gardens clean and walks and lawns clean. Mother told us (on a number of occasions) that one of her jobs as a girl was to pick up sticks in the lawn weekly. This was to be done on Thursday since it was especially important to have the lawn picked up for Sunday and it was done Thursday because it might rain on Saturday or even Friday. The reason for this is that their home was close to the Mennonite Church and people would walk by their home on Sunday mornings.

Mother loved to cook and clean and entertain. Father loved to ask people to come and be entertained. Mother informed the *LaGrange Standard* whenever we had interesting company either in-town or out-of-town. The *Standard*, small town paper that it was, printed it all so that the whole world (at least in LaGrange County) knew who was at our home for Friday dinner. Ruth was surprised after her first visit to LaGrange that her name was in the paper.

Father took care of all things outdoors. Mother took care of all things indoors. She did all of the cleaning and washing and cooking. She also talked on the phone.

She especially talked on the phone. Primarily to Selma, her twin sister in Berne. It was usually at night, after 11:00 PM when the rates were cheaper. I would hear her when I was in bed. She would be laughing and gossiping and talking about birds and church and dresses worn and who knows what. Every other month or so there would be a plaintive cry, "Edna" from Father's study. Father had received the phone bill and wondered how two people could talk so long. Later, when Mother went back to teaching she explained she was doing it so she could talk on the phone whenever she wanted.

From Shipshewana we moved to Millersburg in1935, where Father was principal for two years, and then to LaGrange in 1937 when Father became the County Extension Agent. He was very much pleased to have been selected. He was back in his home county, close to the farm (where he grew up), and in an area where he already had many friends.

No matter where we lived, Mother's heart was always in Berne. Sometimes it showed itself in strange ways, like in her devotion to Dr. Reusser. Dr. Reusser had been the family doctor from 1899 on. I believe he delivered Mother and her sisters. For sure he delivered all of Mother's children. When it was time for any of us to be born Mother went to Berne for Dr. Reusser (to the chagrin of our LaGrange doctor, Dr. Flanagan). Dr. Reusser dispensed pills that were simply numbered: #1, #14, #36. You couldn't get those pills any other place. If you had a headache you took #1; for a fever, #32; for stomach disorder, #45. We liked them because they tasted like sugar. Once as a kid I got a toothache while I was in Berne. Mother did not send me to a dentist but to Dr. Reusser. He looked at the tooth; went out of the room, came back, said "open," clamped onto the tooth with a pair of garage pliers and yanked. No fooling around with Dr. Reusser. When he died in 1956 at the age of 82 after 57 years of doctoring and after he had delivered 4,500 babies, we cut our vacation short in Wisconsin to attend the funeral.

In LaGrange, religion came to the forefront once again. In Millersburg my parents joined the Lutheran Church. When the Lutheran minister in LaGrange came to call he made the bad mistake of questioning my salvation when he learned I had not been baptized. By Mother's account that doomed it for the Lutherans. Much better to be Methodists, who also baptized infants but who didn't seem to care that much, than Lutherans who cared greatly. Obviously Mother believed in believer's baptism. It occurred to me later that since my Aunt Selma said I accepted Jesus at age 3 ½, about the time we moved to LaGrange (I have no memory of this), that I could have taken the vows and been baptized with believer's baptism. But who knows what kind of Lutherans we would have made.

I have reason to believe I had an important part to play in the next religious development. Until LaGrange there was no reason to believe that Mother was ever unhappy with the Methodist Church or religion in Shipshewana, nor with the Lutheran church in Millersburg. But the LaGrange Methodist Church was different. LaGrange was the county seat and the Methodist Church the prestige church in the county. Doctors and lawyers and business people went there, and their religion, while genuine, was not given to weeping for the lost or doing evangelism on the street corners or getting excited about the Second Coming of Christ.

More significantly, my parents became active in the LaGrange church just about the time theological modernism was taking over Methodism. Modernism was not particularly evident in the preachers' sermons, nor in the missionary programs, nor in the Women's group. But it was evident in the Sunday school curriculum materials, especially in the materials for four-year olds.

We arrived in LaGrange in 1937. That same year Ethel L. Smither published the textbook *The Use of the Bible With Children* as the teaching philosophy for Methodist Sunday schools. The book made it plain it was "official" and "approved," not the thinking of one person but of the Methodist Church. According to Smither the times called for "universal reconstruction"—the old ways were not adequate; new ways must prevail. The learning of facts, doctrine, and Bible stories was no longer acceptable in Christian education. What was acceptable was having "vital experiences" and associating them with the Bible. The purpose of Christian education was not to impart knowledge about God or the Bible or salvation, but character growth and personality development.

According to Smither, when the Bible was used with young children (with the comment that the Bible was not God's only revelation) the teacher should start with incidents from the life and teachings of Jesus. Other Bible material was unsuitable for children, such as miracles or any portrayal of Jesus on the cross. Stories should only be told that reflected a spirit of love, unselfishness, and purity. This effectively ruled out the entire Old Testament. Bible story books were to be avoided since they suggested literalistic ideas that would confuse children when they got older. Easter was more about new life evidenced in spring rather than about dead bodies coming to life.

I am convinced very few people in the LaGrange congregation, or most other Methodist congregations, were aware of how totally foreign these ideas were to historic Christian faith. But my mother knew, or at least she sensed something did not square with the faith as she knew it. I wasn't in on any of the discussions, which were mostly with her family, but I am aware of a letter sent from California by a great-aunt and that my Bible training was a reason for alarm. If my great-aunt, whom I had never met, was concerned, others must have been also.

There were also some theological shifts at the Berne Mennonite Church. The church had always been much more evangelical than other General Conference Mennonite churches. Union meetings dating to the early 1900s had brought to town some of the major fundamentalist preachers of the times. In 1930 a new minister, Cornelius Suckau, introduced the congregation to dispensationalism. A number of people bought in, including Uncle Wilbur, married to Selma, Mother's twin sister, and some of his family.

Uncle Wilbur never called it dispensationalism. To him it was fundamental Biblical Christianity. But it was more than fundamental Christianiaty. It was pre-tribulational, pre-millennial, Calvinistic, fundamentalist Christianity, complete with C. I.

Scofield and the Scofield Bible, Moody Bible Institute, Winona Lake Bible Conference, and the religious wars of the 1920s, 30s, and 40s. Dispensationalism would soon capture a large part of the evangelical world, though most Christians were in a haze as to what the implications of the whole system really were. Part of the whole system was the postulation of an apostate church, which sometimes could mean the Roman Catholic Church, but in our case, the Federal Council of Churches (later the National Council of Churches), and, by extension, liberal denominations like the Methodists.

Thus the Methodists became increasingly suspect, and Mother soon found herself, religiously, an alien in a foreign land. While she did not try to hide her faith, she was not one to lay on her friends expositions on the book of Daniel, the gathering of the Jews to a homeland, and End Times. Meanwhile, my father's relatives, the people in LaGrange, and my parent's many other friends, intelligent people all, were without a clue when it came to the complexities of dispensational theology.

To make sure I (and my sisters to follow) had a proper religious education, Mother enrolled me (and us) in the Berne community Bible school. After public school dismissed in the spring on a Friday in Berne, Bible school started in the same classrooms on Monday. For the children scholars, Bible school was ten years running, in the summer, all morning, five-weeks each summer enrolling up to 700 kids – more actually, than there were in the public school. It was complete with subjects and grades (gold stars, actually). There were no crafts nor Kool-aid nor cookies. I (and then also my sisters) stayed with Aunt Selma and Uncle Wilbur.

At the Berne Bible school we violated every principle of enlightened Methodist, and liberal, Church education. We memorized the Sermon on the Mount, heard Bible stories galore, sang songs about fountains of blood flowing deep and wide, had classes on the Westminster Catechism (because this was a "union" school and the Reformed Church was part of it), spoke freely of sin and grace, and salvation, and were rewarded for our efforts with crosses that glowed in the dark.

My father was supportive, but he also thought his side of the family needed to be included in my education. He finally convinced Mother that in the interests of fairness and equal time, if I was spending that much time with her sister, I should be given some time with his sister. So, between my 2nd and 3rd grade, I went to Charleston, Illinois, for five weeks, to stay with my Aunt Gay and Uncle Wayne, and attend summer school at the teacher's college (so the prospective teachers would have someone to teach).

I had a marvelous time at Charleston, freed from all religious constraints. My cousin Wayne, Jr., four years older, was an only child, and had accumulated storehouses of treasures. The closets were stacked high with comic books (which we did not have at our house) and I went through them all (most were from the 1930s and would be valuable if they had been saved). Wayne had toy soldiers, whole sets, complete with battleships, tanks, and guns, and airplanes, and I fought World War I, World War II, and all the wars in between. (Later Aunt Gay bequeathed the soldiers to me for my sons who, with their friends, lost World War III, to say nothing of the collector's value of the sets, when they bombed the armies with rocks.) And, we went to movies, two or three times a week, and saw all of the grade B westerns ever made. I don't think I ever did tell Mother of all the wonderful stuff we did. Aunt Gay gave me a year's subscription to Donald Duck comics for Christmas.

In the second grade Mother started my Bible reading program. I was to start with Genesis 1 and read a chapter a day all the way through to Revelation. Father approved. Anything that involved discipline he was for. Mother explained carefully that the Bible was the Word of God and without error. She was making her fundamentalist points early, but I knew nothing about error except for errors as in English when the teacher marked your paper. I soon had a problem. Words were capitalized I never knew were supposed to be capitalized. There was strange word order ("the gathering together of the waters called the Seas"); and strange words ("everything that creepeth upon the earth"); and strange spelling ("slew"). I somehow dealt with this and made it through Leviticus or Numbers before I started skipping around.

Mother was adamant about the Bible thing. In junior high or so she had Father fix a little shelf by my bedside that was reserved just for my Bible. She could probably tell by the marker whether I was reading or not. At first it was a chapter a day. I remember the day I hit Psalm 119 which went on forever. Later it was to be three chapters a day and five on Sunday. I was reading, but sometimes I got behind and had to read twenty chapters at one sitting.

Meanwhile, in other matters, Mother often did not act like a fundamentalist. Like card-playing. This was definitely forbidden in Berne, but Mother started in Shipshewana and twenty-five years later she was still playing. Eventually, somehow or other this got phased out and by the time I was in college we played card games with Rook cards.

Dancing was another matter. About the time I was in junior high the LaGrange school made the decision to allow dancing at the school and made dancing classes available. Even I was tuned in enough to conservative Christian culture to realize that dancing was supposed to be worldly. This was fine because I hated the idea of dancing. But, lo and behold, Mother made me take the classes. Not only that, she insisted I go to dances. When Patty Miller called me up and asked me to the freshman dance, I responded by saying I had to ask my mother first. With Patty on the phone I argued with my mother about the evils of dancing, but she made me go anyway.

There was no compromise with alcohol. In Berne the only tavern in town seemed a blight on the otherwise sanctified culture. The German Mennonites had used alcohol from the beginning until the American evangelical culture in the early 1900s convinced the town basically to go dry. My cousins would cross the street rather than use the sidewalk in front of the tavern. The only time I ever saw Mother really mad was when Father in our presence drank a beer. We had been invited in Wisconsin to the home of my mother's cousin, Wesley Schnecks and his family, for dinner. Beer was offered as part of the social setting. Father would not, I am convinced, have accepted if it had been one of his relatives. But it was a Berne cousin so he took the glass. On the way home, even in front of her kids, Mother erupted. I don't think Father ever drank again. It was 1946.

Actually, there was another time I remember Mother being really angry. She was obviously not pleased at some of the things I did, but she tended to handle those situations in the Mennonite way: express displeasure without anger. But in the fourth grade I crossed the line. Our music class at school was taught by Mrs. Ferguson, one of Mother's friends. Mrs. Ferguson had the best singers in the back of the room. That was probably not a good idea because it led to an attitude problem (lack of humility). That in turn led to my smarting off (from the back of the room) about something or other. Mrs. Ferguson came back and grabbed me by the arm and dressed me down. No adult had ever done that to me before (I was used to the Mennonite way—no corporal punishment). I then decided I would not sing for Mrs. Ferguson again. She moved me to the front but still I refused. All would have been fine but I had not counted on the report card. I got a C in music.

It was not a pretty scene at home when Mother saw that card. Mother went into a real for sure rant. The result of that was I sang again and got moved to the back of the room. I'm not sure how it relates (but I believe it does somehow), but several months later Mrs. Ferguson gave me (as a fourth grader) a lead part in the grade school musical.

Meanwhile the Methodist Church was bothering Mother more and more. Mother definitely wanted to switch churches to a more fundamental church but there were no options. Presbyterians or Lutherans did not qualify. The Church of God was a different group (class) of people. Furthermore, they were excitable which did not fit Mother's taste. In addition, and mostly, Father would never stand for a switch. He was a happy Methodist by this time. He was faithful and respected and was not pushed beyond his tolerance level in matters religious.

Then, an opportunity came in 1950. Father was offered the county agent's job in DeKalb County. Auburn was the county seat. It was a better job and more money. But it meant moving, leaving Father's home county, and starting over. Mother was overjoyed. She already had a Baptist Church picked out. I was devastated. I saw my whole life disintegrating. My home, my paper route, my friends, and my church would be left behind so that we could go to a far country where I knew no one. I protested. I lobbied. I argued. I threw fits. I made my case over and over. Mother made her case and Father was the judge. In the end Father (and we) did not move. I was rescued. It was a near-death experience. Mother would cope.

About that time Mother started the boys' trio: My friends, Glendon Eaton and Daryle Eaton and I. The Eaton brothers could sing and I could sing. This brought out the finest in Mother. In a few months Steve Fisher joined as bass and we were a quartet. Mother planned the practices, picked out the music, helped us get the parts, and even worked on outfits.

We were good. If not good, at least popular. That is, we got asked everywhere, probably because we were cheap (we cost nothing), available, willing, and sometimes entertaining. One of our entertaining appearances was at a county teacher's meeting, a group we stood in some awe of. Our song was "Dem Bones, Dem Bones Dem Dry Bones," which was already a stretch for Daryle, our first tenor. The song starts with the foot bone and the pitch keeps going up until we reach the head. Unfortunately, by accident we started the song three notes too high. Anyone who knew music and knew the song knew catastrophe was coming. We got from the ankle bone to the knee bone to the thigh bones to the hip bone, but we were already topped out and we had shoulder, neck and head bones yet to go. Daryle could not talk for a week.

Over a period of less than three years we sang 352 times. I questioned the numbers until years later Glendon showed me his log (and newspaper clippings). Father didn't know much about music but he was all for the quartet and lined up numbers of appearances. We sang at schools and churches and clubs and contests and before groups we never knew existed. We sang at Purdue Round-up and for 4-H in Chicago. We even sang for the church service at the coliseum at the state fair with 8,000 people there (according to my diary—the figure is susceptible to inflation). At all farm functions we were the 4-H quartet. At all school-related functions we were the high school quartet. At all church functions we were the Methodist quartet, except when we sang at Steve's Lutheran Church (he was always a bit concerned about singing our gospel songs at his liturgical service), then we were the gospel quartet. We joined the barbershop group so sometimes we were the LaGrange boys' barbership quartet. All of this was master-minded by Mother. Mother followed this by organizing groups for my sisters and others in the church.

My last big struggle of wills with Mother was over seminary. She had hoped I would become a Baptist, but by a quirky turn of events (see chapter six) I ended up at Taylor University, a school with Methodist and Holiness roots. It fit me well. I loved all the Methodist churches we attended. Not only that, I had met Ruth by that time and Ruth was not really into the Baptist thing.

I was called into the ministry but where would I preach? In my developing evangelical world Fuller Seminary in California was the place to go. It was also where my friend Ron Woodward was attending. Mother was delighted. Fuller was full of Baptists and other evangelicals. I would never end up Methodist if I went to Fuller. The same sentiment was expressed by the Methodist district superintendent; ("If you go to Fuller don't expect to come back here.")

But there was another option. If I attended the Methodist school, Garrett Biblical Institute in Evanston, I would be close to Ruth (who had one more year at Taylor). Plus I could pastor a student appointment in Indiana. Mother pulled no punches. Garrett was liberal. My faith would be ruined. I was on some prayer lists. I got several letters from well-known fundamentalist pastors. Aunt Selma talked to me, as did my uncle Wilbur. I did not decide until two weeks before school. I would go to Garrett.

Once married, pastoring evangelical churches, and giving Mother enough assurances that my faith was not compromised (in fact, we had some good theological discussions), my parents, my hometown, and all my relatives, on both Mother's side and Father's side, became great sources of encouragement. Our children loved their grandparents.

Mother solved her Methodist problem by supplementing her church experiences with regular visits to a number of other churches. On Sunday evenings and on other occasions Mother and Father could be found in Baptist churches and Missionary churches and Bible churches in the surrounding towns. She added an expensive FM antenna to pull in Moody Bible Institute (WMBI). She taught

Sunday school, played the organ, and did Bible studies.

We celebrated my parents' 50th wedding anniversary on December 31, 1981. It was a marvelous day, but Mother was already suffering from the bone cancer. She died May 31,1982.

The family gathered. The viewing at the funeral home was scheduled for 2:00 on June 2. The family would gather at 1:00. At 12:30 with nothing to do but wait I decided to grab my binoculars and take a short drive into the country to look for birds. I was about one year into a new hobby—bird-watching. Mother had been a bird-watcher for a large part of her life. She and her sisters, and especially Selma, kept lists. They went to Florida so they could watch birds. When we were growing up, driving down the road Mother would slam on the brakes, automatically throw her right arm out (in days before seatbelts) to catch whatever kid was in the front seat–all because she saw or thought she saw a bird. People who told stories about Mother would tell about finding our car on various roads in the county stopped while Mother was chasing a bird.

Mother tried to interest her children with little success. Then, all the sudden, it took. One summer in North Dakota I took Father Unkenholz's binoculars into the pasture and became hooked on bird-watching. I combined this new love with an interest in photography, especially after the purchase of a telephoto lens.

Mother and I had only a year or so to enjoy this hobby together and she was not well during most of that year. But during that year, and before that last year, I heard Mother lament on several different occasions: "Whatever happened to the bluebirds?" When she was growing up there were lots of bluebirds, but now she had not seen a bluebird for years.

I really wasn't too serious about finding birds in that 20 minute drive through the countryside. I believe I was mostly interested in getting out of the house and doing something before having to go to the funeral home.

Then it was there! At the corner of 200 S and 300 E in LaGrange County--a blue flash! The bluest of the blue! The blue which is the standard by which all blues are compared. A male bluebird.He flew to a fence post and sang. Then to a small tree. Then to another fence post, as if posing. I saw why. There was a wood fence post with a hole. The bluebird was feeding young.

But there was another explanation. The bluebird was posing just for me. It was a sign. I felt like I was on holy ground. I felt like Moses must have felt before the burning bush. There was the overwhelming sense of God's presence, as if a voice was speaking: "It's all right." Like John Wesley's last words: "The best of all is that God is with us."

I watched the bluebird until I could wait no more. I went directly to the funeral home. The casket was open. I saw once again the brown spots, but I was aware of blue birds.

The people came. Several hundred people. They gave testimony; they told stories. I always respected my mother but I never suspected how much she had touched lives. Women in her Bible study. Persons who had her in Sunday school. Neigbhorhood kids on Hawpatch now grown up. Relatives. Grandchildren.

I thought of my great-grandmother who prayed for all her descendents to the 3rd and 4th generation, that not one would be lost. I never heard Mother say she was doing the same thing, but I am confident she was.

When our children were still young we would get our family and my sisters' families together over Christmas break or during the summer for a several days' reunion. When that eventually became impossible Ruth and I would gather with Mary Sue and her husband Deac and Ann and her husband Tom. We would laugh and tell stories of Mother and Father and life in LaGrange and the churches we were attending, and our children. Of course our children. By 2009 there were 49 direct descendents: 3 children; 11 grandchildren, and 34 great-grandchildren, and 1 great-great grandchild. Mother knew the first generation and the second generation, but she never had a chance to meet the 3rd generation, or the 4th. It is sad because she would have been so pleased. She would also know that her prayers had been answered. As far as we know, all are saved and on their way home. The bluebird still sings.